4th ACL-SIGSEM Workshop on Prepositions 2007

Held in conjunction with ACL 2007

Prague, Czech Republic
28 June 2007

ISBN: 978-1-61738-525-4

Printed from e-media with permission by:

Curran Associates, Inc.
57 Morehouse Lane
Red Hook, NY 12571
www.proceedings.com

Some format issues inherent in the e-media version may also appear in this print version.

Printed by Curran Associates, Inc. (2010)

Association for Computational Linguistics
209 N. Eighth Street
Stroudsburg, Pennsylvania 18360

Phone: 1-570-476-8006
Fax: 1-570-476-0860

acl@aclweb.org

Introduction

This volume contains the papers presented at the Fourth ACL-SIGSEM Workshop on Prepositions. This workshop is endorsed by the ACL Special Interest Group on Semantics (ACL-SIGSEM), and is hosted in conjunction with ACL 2007, taking place on 28th June, 2007 in Prague, the Czech Republic.

Prepositions, postpositions and other adpositions have received a considerable amount of interest in recent years. Researchers from linguistics, artificial intelligence and psycholinguistics have examined spatial and temporal aspects of prepositions, their cross-linguistic differences, monolingual and cross-linguistic contrasts, the role of prepositions in syntactic alternations and their semantics in situated dialog. In languages like English and German, phrasal verbs have also been the subject of considerable research, ranging from the development of techniques for their automatic extraction from corpora to methods for determining their semantics. In other languages, like Romance languages or Hindi, the focus has been either on the incorporation of the preposition or its inclusion in the prepositional phrase. All these configurations are important both semantically and syntactically in natural language understanding and processing.

This workshop builds on the success of three previous workshops on prepositions (held in Toulouse, 2003, Colchester, 2005 and Trento, 2006) in providing a forum for researchers to present their current work on these areas. The aim of these workshops has been to bring together researchers from a variety of backgrounds to discuss the syntax, semantics, description, representation and cross-linguistic aspects of prepositions in order to promote collaboration.

We received 16 submissions in total. Each submission was reviewed by at least 3 members of the program committee who not only judged each submission but also gave detailed comments to the authors. Of the received papers 8 were selected for presentation in the workshop: 5 as full-length 8-page papers, and 3 as 6-page short papers.

These eight papers deal with prepositions in six languages (English, French, German, Hindu, Italian and Telugu) and they address applications as diverse as generating route descriptions, grammar checking, and machine translation. The present proceedings thus contain work on:

- investigating determinerless prepositional phrases in German and measuring their productivity with a mathematical approach [Dmges et al.]
- a corpus study to infer the semantics of temporal prepositions in Italian [Caselli and Quochi]
- language technology-oriented lexicography for French prepositions (merging information from different sources and re-structuring them) [Fort and Guillaume]
- an empirical evaluation of geometric constraints on the interpretation of projective English prepositions [Hying] and, in related research, landmark classifications based on English prepositions towards an improved generation of route descriptions [Furlan et al.]
- checking correct preposition usage for English by modeling their contexts with feature vectors [De Felice and Pulman] and by using a maximum entropy classifier combined with rule-based filters [Chodorov et al.]

- the prediction of the correct preposition in English to Hindu and Telugu machine translation [Husain et al.]

We would like to thank all the authors for sharing their research and the members of the program committee for their careful reviews and useful comments to the authors. We would also like to thank Timothy Baldwin and Valia Kordoni for their advice in the planing stages of this workshop, and the ACL 2007 organising committee and workshop coordinators for making this workshop possible.

Fintan Costello, John Kelleher and Martin Volk

May 2007

Organizers

Organizers:

Fintan Costello, University College Dublin, Ireland
John Kelleher, Dublin Institue of Technology, Ireland
Martin Volk, Stockholms Universitet, Sweden

Program Committee:

Boban Arsenijevic, University of Leiden, Netherlands
Doug Arnold, University of Essex, UK
Timothy Baldwin, University of Melbourne, Australia
Collin Baker, University of California Berkeley, USA
John Beavers, Georgetown University, USA
Nicoletta Calzolari,Istituto di Linguistica Computazionale, Italy
Markus Egg, University of Groningen, The Netherlands
Tracy Holloway King, PARC, USA
Valia Kordoni, Saarland University, Germany
Ken Litkowski, CL Research, USA
Tom O'Hara, Convera Inc., USA
Patrick Saint-Dizier, IRIT-Toulouse, France
Hidetosi Sirai, Chukyo University, Japan
Beata Trawinski, University of Tbingen, Germany
Jesse Tseng, Loria, France
Aline Villavicencio, Federal University of Rio Grande do Sul, Brazil
Paul Watts, University College Dublin, Ireland
Feiyu Xu, DFKI, Germany
Joost Zwarts, Utrecht University, The Netherlands

Table of Contents

Conference Program

Thursday 28th June, 2007

2:30–2:45	Opening Remarks
	Session 1: Prepositions in Space
2:45–3:10	*A Corpus-Based Analysis of Geometric Constraints on Projective Prepositions* Christian Hying
3:10–3:35	*Landmark Classification for Route Directions* Aidan Furlan, Timothy Baldwin and Alex Klippel
3:35–4:00	Coffee break
	Session 2: Prepositions in Language
4:00–4:25	*PrepLex: A Lexicon of French Prepositions for Parsing* Karën Fort and Bruno Guillaume
4:25–4:50	*Detection of Grammatical Errors Involving Prepositions* Martin Chodorow, Joel Tetreault and Na-Rae Han
4:50–5:15	*Measuring the Productivity of Determinerless PPs* Florian Dömges, Tibor Kiss, Antje Müller and Claudia Roch
5:15–5:20	Break
	Session 3: Short talks
5:20–5:40	*Inferring the Semantics of Temporal Prepositions in Italian* Tommaso Caselli and Valeria Quochi
5:40–6:00	*Automatically Acquiring Models of Preposition Use* Rachele De Felice and Stephen Pulman
6:00–6:20	*Simple Preposition Correspondence: A Problem in English to Indian Language Machine Translation* Samar Husain, Dipti Misra Sharma and Manohar Reddy
6:20–6:30	Closing Remarks

A Corpus-based Analysis of Geometric Constraints on Projective Prepositions

Christian Hying
IMS, Universität Stuttgart
Azenbergstr. 12
70174 Stuttgart
Germany
christian.hying@ims.uni-stuttgart.de

Abstract

This paper presents a corpus-based method for automatic evaluation of geometric constraints on projective prepositions. The method is used to find an appropriate model of geometric constraints for a two-dimensional domain. Two simple models are evaluated against the uses of projective prepositions in a corpus of natural language dialogues to find the best parameters of these models. Both models cover more than 96% of the data correctly. An extra treatment of negative uses of projective prepositions (e.g. *A* is not above *B*) improves both models getting close to full coverage.

1 Introduction

This paper describes an empirical approach to finding an appropriate model of geometric constraints of projective prepositions with respect to a domain that is implicitly given by a corpus. We examine uses of the projective prepositions *above*, *below*, *to the right of*, *to the left of* and other projective prepositions whose orientation is aligned with one of the former, when they describe the location of an object relative to another object in two-dimensional space, see for example (1) and (2) relating to Figure 1:

(1) The circle is *to the right of* the rectangle.

(2) The circle is **not** *to the left of* the rectangle.

Henceforth, the term *located object* (LO) will be used to refer to the object whose location is specified and the term *reference object* (RO) to refer to the object relative to which the location is specified.

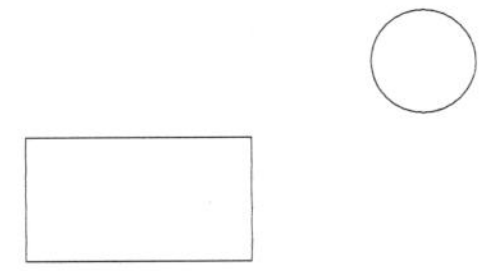

Figure 1: Example of a spatial scene.

In the examples, the *located object* is the circle in Figure 1 and the *reference object* is the rectangle. The notion *projective term* refers to the word of a projective preposition that determines the direction, e.g. the word *right* for the projective preposition *to the right of*. Let us call the use of the projective prepositions *positive use* when it is used in default context as in (1) and *negative use* when it is embedded under negation as in (2).

Geometric constraints that are associated with projective prepositions need to be such that they are met by positive uses such as (1) and violated by negative uses such as (2). Given that these sentences are appropriate uses to describe Figure 1, the spatial scene should meet the constraints that are associated with *to the right of* and violate the constraints of *to the left of*. It is obvious that this dual question of true or false invokes the issue of vagueness: We may find utterances describing a particular spatial scene and also their negations describing the same scene. For example, the following positive use of *above* may be appropriate to describe the spatial scene above – *The circle is above the rectangle* – but also the corresponding negative use in the sentence *The circle is not above the rectangle*.

We collect empirical evidence of uses of projective prepositions from the *HCRC Map Task* corpus (Anderson et al., 1991) – a corpus of human-human

Proceedings of the 4th ACL-SIGSEM Workshop on Prepositions, pages 1–8,
Prague, Czech Republic, June 2007.

dialogues. In contrast to other approaches that report empirical studies on geometric conditions of projective prepositions (Kelleher, 2003; Crawford et al., 2000; Logan and Sadler, 1996; Gapp, 1995; Abella, 1995) the resource used in this paper enables us to study their use in conversation.

This paper presents a new method for automatic evaluation of geometric constraints on projective prepositions with corpus data. We use this method to study the use of projective prepositions in human-human conversations and apply it to two models of geometric constraints with different parameters in order to evaluate the coverage for each parameter. A detailed analysis of incorrect cases leads us to a separate treatment of negative uses.

2 Related Work

This section introduces two types of spatial orientation relations that we are going to use as geometric constraints for projective prepositions in Section 4.

Orientation relations are defined with respect to a *frame of reference* that defines the actual alignment of directions (Levinson, 2003). The present study is carried out under the assumption of a fixed frame of reference such that the maps that are used as spatial data define the reference directions for *above*, *below*, *right*, and *left*. Although projective prepositions are in general sensitive to extra-geometric influences, e.g. dynamic LOs and ROs and functional relations between LO and RO (Coventry and Garrod, 2004), we do not expect that such effects play a role in the data, because the domain is static and it hardly contains any pairs of objects with a functional relationship.

In the literature, we find two paradigms for defining spatial orientation relations: the orthogonal projection paradigm and the angular deviation paradigm. For each paradigm we review a simple model and define different levels of granularity. The limitations of these simple models have been discussed at length, and more complex models have been proposed (Kelleher, 2003; Schmidtke, 2001; Crawford et al., 2000; Matsakis and Wendling, 1999; Fuhr et al., 1995; Abella and Kender, 1993; Wazinski, 1992). Nonetheless, it will turn out that we can find for each simple model a level of granularity which covers more than 96% of the data.

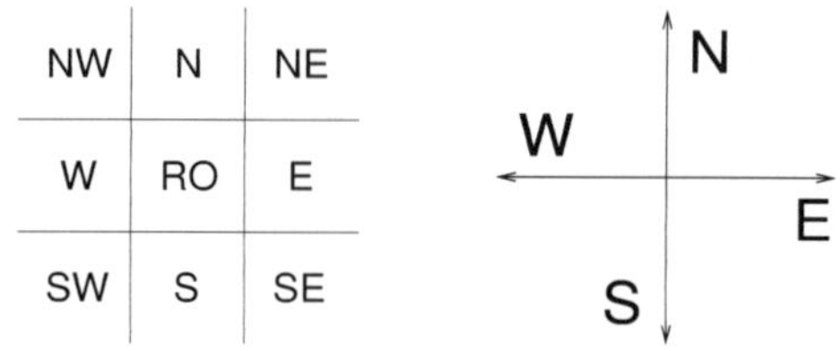

(a) Orthogonal projection model. (b) Angular deviation model.

Figure 2: Definition of directions.

Orthogonal projection. Orthogonal projection models define conditions on intervals that are the result of projecting two-dimensional or three-dimensional objects onto reference axes. (Papadias and Sellis, 1994), for example, define an orthogonal projection model with a horizontal and a vertical axis. Objects are represented by their projection onto these axes or, more illustrative, by bounding boxes. A bounding box of an object is the minimal rectangle with vertical and horizontal sides that contains the object. Lines which are defined by the sides of the bounding box of the reference object divide the space into nine regions. We refer to the regions around the bounding box of the reference object by means of the cardinal directions (*N,S,E,W,NW,NE,SW,SE*) as shown in Figure 2(a).

Let us define two relations OV and INC for expressing overlap and complete inclusion. A region A overlaps with a region B if and only if their intersection is not empty. A region A is completely included in B if and only if their intersection yields A:

(3) $OV(A, B) \Leftrightarrow A \cap B \neq \emptyset$ (*overlap*)
$INC(A, B) \Leftrightarrow A \cap B = A$ (*inclusion*)

The spatial orientation relations between LO and RO presented below are defined in terms of overlap and complete inclusion of LO with the nine regions around RO defined by the model. We exemplify the specification for the direction *north* using the auxiliary regions NHP and NXHP, where NHP $= NW \cup N \cup NE$ is the half-plane consisting of all northern regions and NXHP $=$ NHP $\cup W \cup RO \cup E$ is the (extended) half-plane which consists of all but the southern regions. For each orientation we define different levels of granularity – increasing index indicates wider interpretation. The idea is that relations on OP0 are as strict as possible and on OP7 as wide as possible. On granularity level OP0, the relation $north^0_{op}(LO, RO)$ is true if LO is completely included in the N-region. The predicate on the next granularity level is true if LO overlaps with the given N-region and is included in the northern half-plane NHP. Granularity level OP2 only requires inclusion in NHP. OP3 requires overlap with NHP and inclusion in the extended half-plane NXHP. On level OP4 the relation is true if LO is included in the extended half-plane NXHP. Relations on OP5 require overlap of LO with NXHP and LO must not overlap with S. On OP6 $north^6_{op}(LO, RO)$ is true if the LO does not overlap with S and on OP7 it is true if LO is not completely included in S. The same patterns apply to the relations $south^n_{op}$, $west^n_{op}$, and $east^n_{op}$.

OP0: $north^0_{op}(LO, RO) \Leftrightarrow INC(LO, N)$
OP1: $north^1_{op}(LO, RO) \Leftrightarrow OV(LO, N) \wedge INC(LO, \texttt{NHP})$
OP2: $north^2_{op}(LO, RO) \Leftrightarrow INC(LO, \texttt{NHP})$
OP3: $north^3_{op}(LO, RO) \Leftrightarrow$
$OV(LO, \texttt{NHP}) \wedge INC(LO, \texttt{NXHP})$
OP4: $north^4_{op}(LO, RO) \Leftrightarrow INC(LO, \texttt{NXHP})$
OP5: $north^5_{op}(LO, RO) \Leftrightarrow$
$OV(LO, \texttt{NXHP}) \wedge INC(LO, \texttt{NXHP} \cup SW \cup SE)$
OP6: $north^6_{op}(LO, RO) \Leftrightarrow INC(LO, \texttt{NXHP} \cup SW \cup SE)$
OP7: $north^7_{op}(LO, RO) \Leftrightarrow OV(LO, \texttt{NXHP} \cup SW \cup SE)$

Note, that on granularity levels OP0 to OP3 opposite relations such as $north$ and $south$ are disjoint. Their extensions overlap on levels OP4 to OP7.

Angular deviation. Angular deviation models define conditions on one or more angles that represent how much LO deviates from a reference direction from the perspective of RO. In two-dimensional space there are four reference directions corresponding to the cardinal directions: $\vec{N}$, $\vec{S}$, $\vec{E}$, and $\vec{W}$. They are aligned with the vertical axis and the horizontal axis, respectively, as shown in Figure 2(b). Like the models presented in (Hernandez, 1994; Gapp, 1994) we use centroids to determine one single angle between RO and LO. Let the function $c(\cdot)$ return the centroid of its argument and let $\vec{o}$ be a vector from the centroid of the reference object to the centroid of the located object.

(4) $\vec{o} = \overrightarrow{c(RO)c(LO)}$

The angle between two vectors $\vec{a}$ and $\vec{b}$ is represented as $\angle(\vec{a}, \vec{b})$ and the angular deviation of $\vec{a}$ from the direction given by $\vec{b}$ is represented as $|\angle(\vec{a}, \vec{b})|$.

Orientation relations are defined via inequality conditions specifying that the deviation of the angle $\vec{o}$ from the corresponding reference direction is below or equal to a threshold. The threshold is defined as the granularity level multiplied by 10 degrees. We define 19 granularity levels ADn from n=0 to n=18 according to the pattern shown in (5). The same patterns with the reference directions $\vec{S}$, $\vec{W}$, and $\vec{E}$ apply to the relations $south^n_{ad}$, $west^n_{ad}$, and $east^n_{ad}$, respectively.

(5) ADn: $north^n_{ad}(LO, RO) \Leftrightarrow |\angle(\vec{N}, \vec{o})| \leq (n \cdot 10°)$

Note, that opposite relations such as $north$ and $south$ are disjoint on the levels from AD0 to AD8 and overlap from AD9 to AD18.

3 Data

This section describes the data that is used for the analysis of the semantics of projective prepositions. The data is an exhaustive collection of uses of projective prepositions occurring in the *HCRC Map Task* corpus (Anderson et al., 1991) where the speakers describe the location of a two-dimensional object relative to another two-dimensional object. The *HCRC Map Task* corpus is a collection of route description dialogues where one participant tries to explain a route printed on a map to another participant. It contains transcriptions of 128 dialogues which were recorded with 32 subjects. The maps are schematic maps containing line drawings of objects, so called *landmarks*. Examples of sections of the maps are shown in Section 5. The participants cannot see each other's maps so that the task can be accomplished only by means of what the participants say to one another. The two maps that are used for one dialogue are not exactly identical because not all landmarks have an identical counterpart on the other map. Therefore, the participants align their information about the maps by describing the location of landmarks.

TERM	Frequency	TERM	Frequency
above	87	under	5
left	86	up	5
below	77	west	3
right	65	north	2
underneath	52	south	2
beneath	7	east	1
bottom	7	upwards	1
top	7	over	1
down	5		

Table 1: Frequency of projective terms.

The present study selects those descriptions from the corpus that satisfy the following requirements:

Requirements:
(i) The description describes the location of one landmark relative to exactly one other landmark.
(ii) The description contains a projective preposition that is associated with one of the four cardinal directions from Figure 2(b).
(iii) The description does not contain any modifiers.

After having removed duplicates of descriptions occurring in the same dialogue, the set of data consists of 734 different uses of projective prepositions. 324 uses are filtered out by condition (iii) because they contain modifiers such as hedges (e.g. *just*), direction modifiers (e.g. *straight*), and distance modifiers (e.g. *2 cm*). The remaining set of data consists of 410 different uses of unmodified projective prepositions which further divides into 389 positive uses and 21 negative uses. Table 1 shows all projective terms ordered by frequency.

Spatial data. The corpus is supplemented by electronic copies of the maps that the participants have used. We created geometric representations of each map by redrawing the shape of each landmark and representing it as a closed polygon at the same location as the original landmark. All polygons are associated with unique identifiers. Let us define a function $polygon$ that yields the polygon definition for each landmark. Given that l is an identifier of a landmark and m an identifier of a map, the expression $polygon(l, m)$ returns the definition of the corresponding polygon.

Annotations. We identify all descriptions in the corpus that satisfy the requirements specified above. Then we mark the corresponding projective prepositions in the corpus and annotate them with the following type of information:

(6)
$$\begin{bmatrix} \text{TERM} & : \text{Projective Term} \\ \text{DIAL} & : \text{Dialogue Identifier} \\ \text{MAP} & : \text{Map Identifier} \\ \text{LO} & : \text{Landmark Identifier} \\ \text{RO} & : \text{Landmark Identifier} \\ \text{INT} & : (\texttt{pos} \mid \texttt{neg}) \end{bmatrix}$$

The feature `TERM` denotes the projective term. The feature `DIAL` holds a symbol that uniquely identifies the dialogue which the corresponding utterance occurs in. The feature `MAP` specifies the map which the corresponding utterance describes a part of. The features `LO` for located object and `RO` for reference object hold symbols that uniquely identify landmarks. Finally, the feature `INT` determines the way how to interpret the whole feature structure. It accepts one of the values `pos` and `neg`. The value `pos` indicates positive use of the projective preposition in the given utterance from the corpus: The feature structure is interpreted as the statement that the participant of dialogue `DIAL` who has map `MAP` produced utterances where the location of `LO` relative to `RO` on map `MAP` can be described correctly by the preposition in question. The value `neg` indicates a negative use of the preposition: The feature structure is interpreted as the statement that the participant of dialogue `DIAL` who has map `MAP` produced utterances where the *negation of the preposition* used is appropriate to describe the location of `LO` relative to `RO` on map `MAP`. In the corpus we find cases of explicit and implicit negation. The following two examples show cases of explicit negation.

(7) X is not below Y.

(8) A: Is X below Y?
B: No.

In the first example, the speaker makes a statement and uses a negated prepositional phrase. In the second example, the negation is triggered by a negative response to a question.

Implicit negations are triggered by rejections of alternatives. In the following example, participant A asks B about the truth of alternatives. If B chooses one alternative the others are rejected as incorrect:

(9) A: Is X above or below Y?
B: It's above.

Participant B states that the first alternative *X is above Y* is correct and thereby implicitly rejects the other alternative *X is below Y*.

4 Automatic Evaluation of Geometric Constraints on Projective Prepositions

This section describes a method of automatic evaluation of geometric constraints on projective prepositions with respect to the data described in the previous section.

For each level of granularity of the spatial orientation relations defined in Section 2 we define a model-theoretic semantics that maps projective prepositions onto truth conditions that are expressed in terms of these spatial orientation relations. In general, truth conditions determine the truth of a natural language expression with respect to a particular model of a situation. Applied to data used in this study this means that the truth conditions determine the applicability of projective prepositions with respect to a pair of landmarks that appear on the same map.

Semantics. For each projective preposition we define as many meanings as we have defined levels of granularity of spatial orientation relations in Section 2. We define a semantics on feature structure representations (6). Given the model α and the granularity level n we map a feature structure f onto the truth condition shown in (a) if $f.INT$=`pos` and onto (b) otherwise:

Let f be a feature structure of type (6), $\pi_{lo} = polygon(f.LO, f.MAP)$, and $\pi_{ro} = polygon(f.RO, f.MAP))$, then
(a) $||f.TERM||^n_\alpha(\pi_{lo}, \pi_{ro})$ if $f.INT$=`pos`;
(b) $\neg||f.TERM||^n_\alpha(\pi_{lo}, \pi_{ro})$ if $f.INT$=`neg`.

As said above, the function $polygon(\cdot,\cdot)$ yields a geometric representation of the landmark specified by a landmark identifer and a map identifier. The term $||f.TERM||^n_\alpha$ denotes the mapping of a projective term from Table 1 onto a spatial relation with the account α and the granularity level n. For example, the projective terms *above*, *top*, *up*, *upwards*, *over*, and *north* are all mapped onto $north^n_\alpha$-relations.[1] For example, if we evaluate the account using orthogonal projection and granularity level 0 the feature structure shown in (10) is mapped onto the formula $\neg north^0_{op}(\pi_1, \pi_2)$ where π_1 and π_2 are the polygons determined by `LO` and `RO`, respectively.

level	+pos	-pos	+neg	-neg	corr
OP0	79	310	21	0	100
OP1	249	140	21	0	270
OP2	346	43	19	2	365
OP3	376	13	16	5	392
OP4	385	4	11	10	396
OP5	386	3	7	14	393
OP6	387	2	2	19	389
OP7	389	0	0	21	389

Table 2: Results of the orthogonal projection models.

(10)

TERM	= above
DIAL	= d0
MAP	= m2f
LO	= m2_manned_fort
RO	= m2_rapids
INT	= `neg`

Automatic evaluation. We evaluate a semantics of projective prepositions by automatically computing truth conditions for each feature structure in the data and evaluating it with the corresponding geometric representations of RO and LO. If the truth value is *true* and the feature structure specifies positive use (*i.e.* `INT = pos`), then in this case the semantics is correct. Likewise, if the truth value is *false* and the data specifies negative use (`INT = neg`) the semantics is correct. In all other cases there is a mismatch between the semantics and the feature structure, so that the corresponding use of a projective preposition provides negative empirical evidence against the semantics.

5 Results and Discussion

The results of the evaluation are shown in Table 2 and Table 3. It comprises the evaluation of 27 semantic accounts corresponding to 8 levels of granularity of the orthogonal projection model (OP0 to

[1](O'Keefe, 1996) suggests that distinct projective prepositions can be associated with different levels of granularity, for example, *above* and *up*. For the present study the data is too sparse to compare such differences.

level	+pos	-pos	+neg	-neg	corr
AD0	0	389	21	0	21
AD1	116	273	21	0	137
AD2	179	210	21	0	200
AD3	250	139	21	0	271
AD4	291	98	21	0	312
AD5	320	69	21	0	341
AD6	347	42	20	1	367
AD7	370	19	18	3	388
AD8	382	7	17	4	399
AD9	385	4	14	7	399
AD10	386	3	12	9	398
AD11	386	3	10	11	396
AD12	386	3	7	14	393
AD13	386	3	5	16	391
AD14	387	2	5	16	392
AD15	388	1	4	17	392
AD16	388	1	3	18	391
AD17	388	1	1	20	389
AD18	389	0	0	21	389

Table 3: Results of the angular deviation models.

OP7) and 19 levels of granularity of the angular deviation model with thresholds from 0° (AD0) to 180° (AD18). The first column specifies the granularity level used. The evaluation of positive uses of projective prepositions is listed in the second and third column, the results for negative uses in the fourth and fifth column. The columns *+pos* and *+neg* report the number of correct cases in which the truth conditions are consistent with the value of the `INT` feature. The number of all correct cases is the sum of *+pos* and *+neg* and is printed in the last column with the label *corr*. The remaining columns *-pos* and *-neg* report incorrect truth conditions for positive and negative uses, respectively.

Orthogonal projection. Over all orthogonal projection models OP4 (included in extended half-plane) correctly covers a maximum number of 396 cases (96.6%).

For a more detailed analysis aiming at full coverage we take a closer look at the errors: there are 4 positive uses for which OP4 provides an incorrect semantics. The corpus reveals that three of these uses are not covered by OP4 because the speakers confused left and right. This confusion is apparent either because it is corrected by the speaker at a later point in the dialogue or because the use is obviously wrong. The remaining case is given by the following part of the corpus relating to Figure 3:

(11) *dialogue q4ec3, utterance 174f*

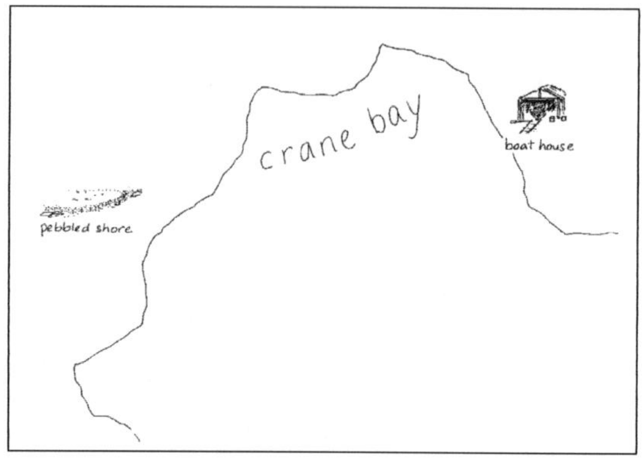

Figure 3: Pebbled shore, crane bay, and boat house.

Figure 4: Disused warehouse and giraffes.

G: have you got anything **below** pebbled shore

F: washed stones and flag ship ... and bay

Note, that Figure 3 does not display the landmarks *washed stones* and *flag ship*. The participant *F* says that *crane bay* is below *pebbled shore*. This case is not captured by OP4 but by OP5 (overlap with extended half-plane).

All negative uses are correctly rejected by OP0 and OP1. The next level OP2 (i.e. completely included in half-plane) does not reject the following two cases:

(12) *dialogue q4nc2, utterance 264f*

G: i don't have a disused warehouse on mine

F: oh right. well it's just parallel to it ... like ... just ehm ... ... well not **underneath** the giraffes ... you know ...

(13) *dialogue q3nc7, utterance 66f*

G: is totem pole **below** the trout farm?

F: no i–, well, it's kind of opposite it

These uses are explicit negations. In (12) F says

Figure 5: Totem pole and trout farm.

that the *warehouse* in Figure 4 is not underneath the *giraffes*. And in (13) F indicates that the *totem pole* is not below the *trout farm* in Figure 5. As said before, OP1 is the most general model that rejects these cases.

To summarise, a semantics that aims at covering all of the *good* data employs OP5 for positive uses and OP1 for negative uses. [2] On level OP5 and to a lesser extent on OP4, the extensions of opposite relations such as *above* and *below* overlap, because all objects that are included in the union of the regions W, RO, and E are both *above* and *below* relative to the reference object. Since on OP4 the overlap is smaller than on OP5 it is better to use OP4 instead. A combination of OP4 for positive uses and OP1 for negative uses still covers almost all of the good data (99.8%).

Angular deviation. Over all angular deviation models AD8 and AD9 correctly cover a maximum number of 399 cases (97.3%).

On level AD9 there are 4 positive uses with an incorrect semantics. Again the same three uses as above are due to confusion of left and right. The remaining use is the following utterance, which relates to the part of a map depicted in Figure 3. The narrowest model that covers this use is AD13:

(14) *dialogue q4ec3, utterance 332*
my boat house is ... down **below** crane bay

All negative uses are correctly rejected by all models from AD0 to AD5. Model AD6 does not predict rejection of the case which has already been described above in (12). AD7 additionally produces two further errors in the following two cases which describe Figure 6(a) and Figure 6(b), respectively.

[2] *Good* data means all data excluding the cases where left and right was confused.

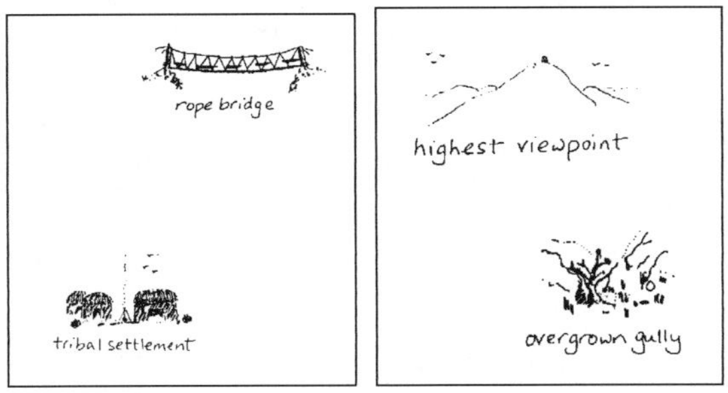

(a) Tribal settlement and rope bridge. (b) Highest viewpoint and overgrown gully

Figure 6: Section of maps 13 and 10.

(15) *dialogue q4ec1, utterance 10f*
F: is it **underneath** the rope bridge or to the **left**?
G: it's **underneath** the rope bridge

(16) *dialogue q4ec8, utterance 41f*
G: and eh to the ... **left** or **right** of highest viewpoint
F: ... it's **beneath** it

These examples show implicit negative uses. The utterances in (15) give rise to the interpretation that the *tribal settlement* is *not* to the left *rope bridge*. And the utterances in (16) imply that the *overgrown gully* is neither to the left nor to the right of the *highest viewpoint*. These three negative uses and again the localisation of the *totem pole* in (13) have not been modelled correctly by the semantics that employs AD8.

To summarise, a semantics aiming to cover all of the *good* data uses AD13 for positive uses and AD5 for negative uses. Considering that the extensions of the opposite relations in AD13 overlap to a great extent, it is better to use a combination of AD9 for positive uses and AD5 for negative uses which still covers all of the good data except one case (99.8%).

If we compare the angular deviation model (AD9/AD5) with the orthogonal projection model (OP4/OP1), the angular deviation model is superior, because in AD9 the extensions of opposite relations such as *above* and *below* only have a very small overlap, namely when the angular deviation is exactly 90°, while in OP4 the overlap is much more significant.

6 Summary and Conclusion

This paper described a method to evaluate geometric constraints on projective prepositions with empirical data extracted from a corpus of human-human conversations. The key feature of the approach is the annotation of projective prepositions in the corpus with links to geometric representations of the objects that the arguments of the prepositions refer to. The data is used to automatically apply and evaluate different granularity levels of a semantics building upon a simple orthogonal projection model and a simple angular deviation model. Both models cover more than 96% of the data correctly. Further refinement shows that the angular deviation model covers the data almost perfectly (99.8%) if we provide an extra treatment for negative uses, so that positive uses are accepted when the angular deviation is below 90° and negative uses are accepted when the angular deviation is greater than 50°.

References

Alicia Abella and John R. Kender. 1993. Qualitatively describing objects using spatial prepositions. In *National Conference on Artificial Intelligence*, pages 536–540.

Alicia Abella. 1995. *From imagery to salience: locative expressions in context*. Ph.D. thesis, Computer Science Department, Columbia Universtity, New York, NY.

A. Anderson, M. Bader, E. Bard, E. Boyle, G. M. Doherty, S. Garrod, S. Isard, J. Kowtko, J. McAllister, J. Miller, C. Sotillo, H. S. Thompson, and R. Weinert. 1991. The HCRC Map Task Corpus. *Language and Speech*, 34(4):351–366.

Kenny Coventry and Simon Garrod. 2004. Towards a classification of extra-geometric influences on the comprehension of spatial prepositions. In *Functional Features in Language and Space*.

L. Elizabeth Crawford, Terry Regier, and Janellen Huttenlocher. 2000. Linguistic and non-linguistic spatial categorization. *Cognition*, 75(3):209–235.

T. Fuhr, G. Socher, C. Scheering, and G. Sagerer. 1995. A three-dimensional spatial model for the interpretation of image data. In *IJCAI-95 Workshop on Representation and Processing of Spatial Expressions*, Montreal, Canada.

Klaus-Peter Gapp. 1994. Basic meanings of spatial relations: computation and evaluation in 3d space. In *AAAI'94: Proceedings of the twelfth national conference on Artificial intelligence (vol. 2)*, pages 1393–1398, Menlo Park, CA, USA. American Association for Artificial Intelligence.

K.-P. Gapp. 1995. An empirically validated model for computing spatial relations. In I. Wachsmuth, C.-R. Rollinger, and W. Brauer, editors, *KI-95: Advances in Artificial Intelligence. 19th German Annual Conference on Artificial Intelligence*, pages 245–256. Springer, Berlin, Heidelberg.

Daniel Hernandez. 1994. *Qualitative Representation of Spatial Knowledge*. Springer-Verlag New York, Inc.

John Kelleher. 2003. *A Perceptually Based Computational Framework for the Interpretation of Spatial Language in 3D Simulated Environments*. Ph.D. thesis, Dublin City University, Dublin.

Stephen C. Levinson. 2003. *Space in Language and Cognition*. Cambridge University Press.

Gordon D. Logan and Daniel D. Sadler. 1996. A computational analysis of the apprehension of spatial relations. In Paul Bloom, Mary A. Peterson, Lynn Nadel, and Merril G. Garrett, editors, *Language and Space*. MIT Press.

Pascal Matsakis and Laurent Wendling. 1999. A new way to represent the relative position between areal objects. *IEEE Transactions on Pattern Analysis and Machine Intelligence*, 21(7):634–643.

John O'Keefe. 1996. The spatial prepositions in English, vector grammar, and the cognitive map theory. In Paul Bloom, Mary A. Peterson, Lynn Nadel, and Merril G. Garrett, editors, *Language and Space*. MIT Press.

Dimitris Papadias and Timos K. Sellis. 1994. Qualitative representation of spatial knowledge in two-dimensional space. *VLDB Journal: Very Large Data Bases*, 3(4):479–516.

Hedda R. Schmidtke. 2001. The house is north of the river: Relative localization of extended objects. In D.R. Montello, editor, *COSIT 2001, LNCS 2205*, pages 415–430.

Peter Wazinski. 1992. Generating spatial descriptions for cross-modal references. In *Proceedings of the third conference on Applied natural language processing*, pages 56–63. Association for Computational Linguistics.

Landmark Classification for Route Directions

Aidan Furlan†, Timothy Baldwin† and Alex Klippel‡

† CSSE
University of Melbourne
VIC 3010, Australia
{afurlan,tim}@csse.unimelb.edu.au

‡ Department of Geography
Penn State University
University Park, PA 16802, USA
klippel@psu.edu

Abstract

In order for automated navigation systems to operate effectively, the route instructions they produce must be clear, concise and easily understood by users. In order to incorporate a landmark within a coherent sentence, it is necessary to first understand how that landmark is conceptualised by travellers — whether it is perceived as point-like, line-like or area-like. This paper investigates the viability of automatically classifying the conceptualisation of landmarks relative to a given city context. We use web data to learn the default conceptualisation of those landmarks, crucially analysing preposition and verb collocations in the classification.

1 Introduction

At present, many navigation systems produce badly-worded and difficult to follow route instructions, which do not closely correspond with the way people give one another directions (Dale et al., 2005). Typically, automated navigation systems give turning instructions with street names as reference points, eg *turn right at Smith St*. By contrast, human-generated route instructions tend to use landmarks in preference to street names as navigational reference points (Michon and Denis, 2001).

According to Allen (1997), landmarks are typically used in route directions in one of two ways—as descriptives, providing a static picture of a spatial scene so that the traveller can verify his or her location along a route, eg *the City Library is on your left*, or to specify or clarify a point on a route at which the traveller must make a choice between multiple pathways, termed choice points or decision points. Route instructions which identify decision points with respect to landmarks have been found to be significantly easier to follow than standard street-based or turn-based route instructions (Michon and Denis, 2001).

This paper goes beyond classical approaches to landmarks that focus on salient point-like objects. Instead, we aim to find appropriate ways of classifying landmarks automatically, based on the way those landmarks are used in spatial sentences on the web: as point-like, linear-like, and area-like objects that structure movement pattern in urban spaces. In particular, we analyse how different prepositions and verbs with pre-classified semantics co-occur with mentions of the landmarks. A preposition such as *through* can be used with reference to a landmark we are conceptualising as an area, but not one we are conceptualising as a point. Landau and Jackendoff (1993) presented an analysis of the spatial properties of commonly used English spatial prepositions, such as *at*, *in* and *to*. This classification used as the basis of a list of prepositions for the present study, grouped according to whether the preposition indicates a point-like, line-like or area-like landmark. In addition, a short list of verbs was compiled based on the verb classes of Levin (1993) and similarly divided into the three conceptual classes.

Each of the verbs and prepositions was combined in turn with a list of landmarks in Melbourne, Australia, to produce a series of spatial phrases such as *at Flinders St Station*. These phrases were then

Proceedings of the 4th ACL-SIGSEM Workshop on Prepositions, pages 9–16,
Prague, Czech Republic, June 2007.

sent to the Google search engine, which determined the approximate number of documents on the web containing that exact phrase. The document counts were then summed over the conceptual categories the prepositions and verbs appeared in — point, line and area. The result of this was a probabilistic categorisation of each landmark, according to its usage in spatial contexts on the web.

Evaluation of the baseline was performed based on annotators' independent judgements of the conceptual class of each of the landmarks, gathered from a web-based annotation interface. It was found that the baseline classification agreed with the gold standard classification 63.8% of the time. A slight improvement on the baseline was achieved via a supervised neural network classifier, which took the web counts as inputs. This classifier agreed with the gold standard 68.5% of the time. As a result of this analysis, a set of systematically ambiguous landmarks was identified, with implications for future landmark classification models.

In the remainder of this paper, we describe background research (Section 2) and then outline our research methodology (Section 3). We then present the results of a series of landmark classification experiments (Section 4), and finally discuss the broader implications of the experiments (Section 5).

2 Background

2.1 Spatial Cognition

Route directions should be designed in such a way as to be quickly and easily comprehended by the traveller (Lovelace et al., 1999). Optimally, route directions should exhibit cognitive adequacy — characterising an external representation of a route (as with a map or route directions) in a way supportive of human spatial cognitive processes and knowledge representation (Klippel, 2003). For this reason, the improvement of route directions requires an investigation into human spatial cognition.

Route instructions which reference landmarks are able to achieve a number of worthwhile goals: they have the effect of increasing the spatial awareness of the recipient by informing them about their surroundings; landmark-referencing route instructions can decrease the cognitive load on the recipient; and it is more natural-sounding to receive route instructions in terms of landmarks.

2.2 Landmark Conceptualisation

In order to provide appropriate landmark-referenced route instructions, it is necessary to understand how landmarks can be used in spatial sentences to locate a trajector. On a geometric level, all landmarks can be considered areas when projected onto a top-down map. However, on a conceptual level, landmarks can be used in a point-like, line-like or area-like manner, depending on their spatial relationship with a route (Hansen et al., 2006).

One possible approach to determining a landmark's conceptual class is to make use of the landmark's geometric context, including its size relative to the route and the number of decision points with which it coincides. However, this approach may have little ecological validity, as people may not in fact conceptualise landmarks as point, line or area based purely on geometry, but also based on pragmatic considerations. For instance, it may be the case that people don't tend to conceptualise Flinders St Station as an area, even though it satisfies the geometric criteria.

2.3 Past Research on Landmark Interpretation

The only research we are aware of which has addressed this same topic of landmark interpretation is that of Tezuka and Tanaka (2005). In an investigation of the spatial use of landmarks in sentences, Tezuka and Tanaka (2005) modified existing web mining methods to include spatial context in order to obtain landmark information.

It is natural to question the appropriateness of web data for research purposes, because web data is inevitably noisy and search engines themselves can introduce certain idiosyncracies which can distort results (Kilgarriff and Grefenstette, 2003). However, the vast amount of data available can nevertheless give better results than more theoretically motivated techniques (Lapata and Keller, 2004). And importantly, the data that can be gleaned from the web does not mirror the view of a single person or a select group, but of the entire global community (or at least the best available representation of it).

3 Methodology

The prepositions and verbs which accompany a landmark in spatial sentences capture that landmark's implicit conceptualisation. We use this implicit conceptualisation, as represented on the web, to develop two automated classification schemes: a simple voting classifier and a neural network classifier. We compile a set of gold standard classifications in order to evaluate the performance of the classifiers.

3.1 Landmarks

A list of 58 landmarks was generated for Melbourne, Australia. The landmarks were chosen to be uniquely identifiable and recognisable by most inhabitants of Melbourne.

3.2 Gold Standard

We had annotators use a web interface to uniquely classify each landmark as either point-, line- or area-like. Each landmark's gold standard category was taken to be the category with the greatest number of annotator votes. Where the annotations were split equally between classes, the maximal geometric class was chosen, which is to say, line was chosen in preference to point, and area was chosen in preference to line. The rationale for this is that, for example, a point-like representation is always recoverable from a landmark nominally classified as an area, but not the other way around. Hence the classification which maintains both pieces of information, that this landmark may be treated as an area or a point, was assigned preferentially to the alternative, that this landmark may only be treated as a point.

Since landmark conceptualisations can depend on the mode of transport involved, annotators were instructed to consider themselves a cyclist who nevertheless behaves like a car by always staying on the street network. The intention was to elicit conceptualisations based on a modality which is intermediate between a car and a pedestrian. Annotators were also asked to indicate their confidence in each annotation.

3.3 Web Mining

We identified a set of prepositions and verbs as indicating a point-like, line-like or area-like representation. The number of documents on the web which were found to contain a particular landmark in point-like, line-like or area-like spatial sentences provided the raw data for our automated classification schemes. The web data thus obtained can be considered an implicit representation of a generalised cognitive model of the landmarks.

Prepositions

Landau and Jackendoff (1993) investigated the use of English spatial prepositions and the requirements they place on the geometric properties of reference objects. This analysis was projected onto the conceptual classes of point, line and area, to form a list of conceptually grouped spatial prepositions. Hence prepositions which require the reference object to be (or contain) a bounded enclosure, such as *inside*, were classified as denoting an area-like landmark; prepositions which require the reference to have an elongated principal axis, such as *along*, were classified as denoting a line-like landmark; and prepositions which place no geometric constraints on the reference object, such as *at*, were classified as denoting a point-like landmark.

The prepositions used were restricted to those which pertain to a horizontal planar geometry compatible with route directions; for example, prepositions which make use of a reference object's vertical axis such as *on top of* and *under* were ignored, as were prepositions denoting contact such as *against*. The preposition *out* was also excluded from the study as it is typically used in non-spatial contexts, and in spatial contexts the reference object is usually covert (eg *he took his wallet out*) (Tyler and Evans, 2003). Conversely, *out of* is frequently spatial and the reference object is overt, so this compound preposition was retained. The complete list of prepositions used in the study is given in Table 1.

Verbs

In addition to the list of prepositions, a list of verbs was created based on the verb classes of Levin (1993), restricted to verbs of inherently directed motion which can be used in a phrase immediately preceding a landmark, such as the verb *pass* in the phrase *pass the MCG*; in other words, the chosen verbs can be used in a way which parallels the use of spatial prepositions, as opposed to verbs such as

Point-like	Line-like	Area-like
across from	along	around
at	alongside	across
after		in
away from		inside (of)
before		into
behind		out of
beside		outside (of)
in front of		through
near		within
next to		without
opposite		
past		
to		
to the left of		
to the right of		
to the side of		
toward		

Table 1: Prepositions used in this research (based on Landau and Jackendoff (1993))

Point-like	Line-like	Area-like
hit	follow	cross
pass		enter
reach		leave

Table 2: Verbs used in this research

proceed, which specify a motion but require a preposition for clarification. This second type of verb is of no interest to the study as they tell us nothing about the conceptualisation of landmarks.

As with the prepositions, the verbs were grouped into the conceptual classes of point, line and area according to the requirements they place on reference objects, including *enter* for an area-like object, *follow* for a line-like object and *pass* for a point-like object. The complete list of verbs used in the study is given in Table 2.

Document Counts

Each of the prepositions and verbs was combined with each of the landmarks to create a cross-product of linguistic chunks, such as *at Queen Victoria Market*, *through Queen Victoria Market*, and so on. Alternative names and common misspellings of the landmark names were taken into account, such as *Flinders St Station*, *Flinders Street Station* and *Flinder's Street Station*. Additionally, three conjugations of each verb were used—present tense non-3rd person singular (eg *reach*), present tense 3rd person singular (eg *reaches*), and past tense (eg *reached*).

Each linguistic chunk was sent in turn to the Google search engine, which determined the approximate number of documents on the web containing that exact phrase. The counts were then summed over the conceptual categories in which each preposition and verb appeared. The result of this was a probabilistic categorisation of each landmark as point, line or area, according to its usage in spatial sentences on the web.

It is difficult to determine the context of sentences using a search engine. It is uncertain whether the documents found by Google use the searched-for linguistic chunks in a spatial context or in some other context. For this reason, each preposition and verb was assigned a weight based on the proportion of occurrences of that word in the Penn Treebank (Marcus et al., 1993) which are labelled with a spatial meaning. This weighting should give an approximation to the proportion of spatial usages of that word on the web.

Automated Classification

As a naive automated classification of the landmarks, the document counts were used to place each landmark in one of the three conceptual classes. Each landmark was placed in the class in which it was found to appear most frequently, based on the classes of the prepositions and verbs with which it appeared on the web. Hence landmarks which appeared more often with a point-like preposition or verb, such as *at* or *pass*, were placed in the point category; landmarks which appeared more often with a line-like preposition or verb, such as *follow*, were placed in the line category; and landmarks which appeared more often with an area-like preposition or verb, such as *around*, were placed in the area category.

As a more sophisticated classification scheme, we developed a supervised artificial neural network classifier. The neural network we developed consisted of a three node input layer, a two node hidden layer and a two node output layer, with learning taking place via the backpropagation algorithm. For each landmark, the percentage of web counts in each of the three conceptual classes was used as the initial activation value of the three nodes in the input layer. The activation of the output nodes was rounded to 1 or 0. The output node activations were used to indicate whether a landmark falls into the point, line or area category — 01 for point, 10 for line and 11 for area. An output of 00 was taken to indicate a failure to classify. The neural network was trained and tested using fourfold cross-validation, with the gold standard classification as the desired output in each case.

4 Results

Five experiments were conducted on the simple voting classifier and the neural network classifier. These experiments used increasingly sophisticated inputs and gold standard measures to try to improve the performance of the classifiers, as measured against the gold standard. The neural network classifier outperformed the voting classifier in all experiments but the final one.

Of the 58 Melbourne landmarks, 27 were classified as points by the majority of annotators, 2 as lines, and 29 as areas. These majority classifications were used as the gold standard. For these classifications, we calculated a kappa statistic of 0.528 (Carletta, 1996). This suggests that the annotation classification task itself was only moderately well-formed, and that the assumption that multiple annotators will classify landmarks in a similar manner does not necessarily hold true.

To determine whether the classifiers were performing at an acceptable level, we established a majority-class baseline: 29 of the 58 landmarks were areas, and hence the majority class classifier has an accuracy of 50%.

The maximum meaningful accuracy that can be achieved by a classifier is limited by the accuracy of the annotations themselves, creating an upper bound for classifier performance. The upper bound was calculated as the mean pairwise inter-annotator agreement, which was determined to be 74.4%.

	Accuracy (%)	E.R.R. (%)
Baseline	50.0	
Voting Classifier	63.8	56.6
Neural Net Classifier	70.0	82.0
Agreement	74.4	

Table 3: Results with simple web counts (Experiment 1)

4.1 Experiment 1

Experiment 1 involved using only the raw web count data as input into the classifiers. The accuracy and error rate reduction (E.R.R.) of the classifiers are given in Table 3.

The neural network classifier produced results slightly better than the simple voting classifier, but with 18 landmarks incorrectly classified by the neural network, there is still plenty of room for improvement. The raw web count data used in this experiment was likely to be biased in favour of certain prepositions and verbs, because some of these words (such as *at* and *in*, which each occur in over 7 billion documents) are much more common than others (such as *beside*, which occurs in just over 50 million documents). This may result in the web counts being unfairly weighted towards one class or another, creating classifier bias.

The simple voting classifier showed a tendency towards point classifications over line or area classifications. The neural network classifier reversed the bias shown by the simple voting classifier, with the area class showing high recall but low precision, resulting in a low recall for the point class. Neither of the two line landmarks were classified correctly; in fact, none of the landmarks were classified as lines.

4.2 Experiment 2

To adjust for the potential bias in preposition and verb use, the web counts were normalised against the prior probabilities of the relevant preposition or verb, by calculating the ratio of the count of each linguistic chunk to the count of its preposition or verb in isolation. The accuracy and error rate reduction of the classifiers are given in Table 4.

Normalising the web counts by the prior probabilities of the prepositions and verbs did not improve the accuracy of the classifiers as expected. The sim-

	Accuracy (%)	E.R.R. (%)
Baseline	50.0	
Voting Classifier	55.2	21.3
Neural Net Classifier	70.0	82.0
Upper	74.4	

Table 4: Results with normalised web counts (Experiment 2)

ple voting classifier reduced in accuracy, while the accuracy of the neural net classifier remained unchanged.

4.3 Experiment 3

As explained in Section 3.2, the annotators who generated the gold standard were required to choose one of point, line or area for each landmark, even if they were unfamiliar with the landmark. Some of these annotators may have been forced to guess the appropriate class. As a result, these annotations may cause the gold standard to lack validity, which could be one of the barriers to classifier improvement.

In this experiment, a more sound gold standard was generated by weighting annotators' classifications by their familiarity with the landmark. The effect of this is that the judgement of an annotator who is very familiar with a landmark outweighs the judgement of an annotator who is less familiar. Experiments 1 and 2 were conducted again based on this new gold standard. These repeated experiments are dubbed Experiments $1'$ and $2'$ respectively. The results of each of the repeated experiments are shown in Table 5.

The simple voting classifier showed improvement using the weighted gold standard, with the accuracies under Experiments $1'$ and $2'$ each exceeding the accuracy of the equivalent experiment using the original gold standard. Experiment $1'$ showed the most improvement for the simple voting classifier, giving an accuracy of 67.2% (only one landmark shy of the 70% accuracy achieved by the neural network classifier in experiment 1).

While landmarks well-known to all are likely to produce consistently valid classifications, and landmarks poorly known to all are likely to produce consistently invalid classifications, regardless of whether a weighting scheme is used, it is the landmarks which are well-known to some and poorly known to others which should have gained the greatest benefit from annotations weighted by familiarity. However, the majority of such landmarks were already being classified correctly by the neural network in both Experiments 1 and 2, which explains why the neural network showed no improvement.

5 Discussion

Surprisingly, the naive conditions in Experiment 1 produced the best overall result, which was a 70% accuracy for the neural network classifier. Although the voting classifier and the neural network classifier produced similar levels of accuracy for many of the experiments, there was very little overlap in the landmarks that were correctly assigned by each classifier. Of the 40 landmarks correctly assigned by the neural network, 18 were incorrectly classified by the voting classifier. Conversely, of the 37 landmarks correctly assigned by the voting classifier, 15 were incorrectly assigned by the neural network. This indicates that the neural net is doing something more sophisticated than simply assigning each landmark to its maximum category.

A rather large subset of the landmarks was found to be consistently misclassified by the neural net, under various training conditions. For a number of these landmarks, the annotators showed strong disagreement and indicated that the landmark is ambiguous, suggesting that there is indeed an inherent ambiguity in the way these landmarks are conceptualised, both between annotators and on the web. Interestingly, all of the hospitals in the landmark list were consistently misclassified. A number of annotators expressed confusion with regard to these landmarks, as to whether the hospital itself or the surrounding gardens should be taken into account. As a result, annotations of the hospitals tended to be split between point and area.

However, some of the landmarks that were misclassified by the neural net were classified consistently by the annotators — for example, GPO was classified as a point by all of the Melbourne annotators. The ambiguity here presumably lies in the web counts, which were not able to detect the same conceptualisation generated by the annotators. One complication with using web counts is the fact

Experiment	Voting Classifier Accuracy (%)	Voting Classifier E.R.R. (%)	Neural Network Classifier Accuracy (%)	Neural Network Classifier E.R.R. (%)
$1'$	67.2	70.5	65.5	63.5
$2'$	58.6	35.2	65.5	63.5

Table 5: Results weighted according to landmark familiarity (Experiments $1'$ and $2'$)

that the data is global in scope, and with a simple abbreviation like GPO, there may well be interference from documents which do not refer to the Melbourne landmark, and in fact may not refer to a landmark or spatial object at all.

One of the underlying assumptions of the study was that all landmarks can be represented as falling into exactly one of the three conceptual classes — point, line or area. This may be an oversimplification. Some landmarks may in fact be more prototypical or ambiguous than others. Certainly, a number of the landmark annotations were split almost equally between point, line and area. It may be that annotators did not or could not take upon themselves the mentality of a cyclist as requested in the annotation instructions, and instead simply conceptualised the landmarks as they usually would, whether that entails a pedestrian or car modality, or some alternative such as a train or tram-like modality. It may also be the case that there are individual differences in the way people conceptualise certain types of landmarks, or indeed space in general, regardless of the modality involved. If this is true, then the low inter-annotator agreement may be a product of these individual differences and not merely an artifact of the experiment design.

In summary, we have proposed a method for classifying landmarks according to whether they are most point-like, line-like or area-like, for use in the generation of route descriptions. Our method relies crucially on analysis of what prepositions and verbs the landmarks co-occur with in web data. In a series of experiments, we showed that we are able to achieve accuracy levels nearing inter-annotator agreement levels for the task.

One simplification made during the course of this study was the treatment of parks and districts as being comparable entities (i.e. area-like landmarks). In fact, a distinction may be made between open areas such as districts, with which the preposition *through* may be used, and closed areas such as parks, for which *through* does not apply for car navigation (although obviously does apply for pedestrian navigation). We hope to take this into account in future work.

Acknowledgments

This research was supported by Australian Research Council DP grant no. DP0770931. The authors wish to thank Lars Kulik for his input into this research.

References

Gary L. Allen. 1997. From knowledge to words to wayfinding: Issues in the production and comprehension of route directions. In *Spatial Information Theory: Cognitive and Computational Foundations of Geographic Information Science (COSIT 1997)*, pages 363–372.

Jean Carletta. 1996. Assessing agreement on classification tasks: the kappa statistic. *Computational Linguistics*, 22(2):249–254.

Robert Dale, Sabine Geldof, and Jean-Philippe Prost. 2005. Using natural language generation in automatic route description. *Journal of Research and Practice in Information Technology*, 37(1):89–105.

Stefan Hansen, Kai-Florian Richter, and Alexander Klippel. 2006. Landmarks in OpenLS — a data structure for cognitive ergonomic route directions. In *Geographic Information Science — Fourth International Conference, GIScience 2006*, pages 128–144.

Adam Kilgarriff and Gregory Grefenstette. 2003. Introduction to the special issue on the web as corpus. *Computational Linguistics*, 29(3):333–347.

Alexander Klippel. 2003. *Wayfinding Choremes: Conceptualizing Wayfinding and Route Direction Elements*. Ph.D. thesis, Universitt Bremen.

Barbara Landau and Ray Jackendoff. 1993. "what" and "where" in spatial cognition. *Behavioral and Brain Sciences*, 16:217–65.

Mirella Lapata and Frank Keller. 2004. The web as a baseline: Evaluating the performance of unsupervised web-based models for a range of nlp tasks. In *Proceedings of the Human Language Technology Conference of the North American Chapter of the Association for Computational Linguistics*, pages 121–128.

Beth Levin. 1993. *English Verb Classes and Alternations. A Preliminary Investigation*. University of Chicago Press, Chicago.

Kirstin Lovelace, Mary Hegarty, and Daniel R. Montello. 1999. Elements of good route directions in familiar and unfamiliar environments. In *Spatial Information Theory: Cognitive and Computational Foundations of Geographic Information Science (COSIT 1999)*, pages 65–82, Stade, Germany.

Mitchell P. Marcus, Beatrice Santorini, and Mary Ann Marcinkiewicz. 1993. Building a large annotated corpus of English: the Penn treebank. *Computational Linguistics*, 19(2):313–30.

Pierre-Emmanuel Michon and Michel Denis. 2001. When and why are visual landmarks used in giving directions? In *Spatial Information Theory: Cognitive and Computational Foundations of Geographic Information Science (COSIT 2001)*, pages 292–305, Morro Bay, USA.

Taro Tezuka and Katsumi Tanaka. 2005. Landmark extraction: A web mining approach. In *Spatial Information Theory: Cognitive and Computational Foundations of Geographic Information Science (COSIT 2005)*, pages 379–396, Ellicottville, USA.

Andrea Tyler and Vyvyan Evans. 2003. *Lexical meaning and experience: the semantics of English prepositions*. Cambridge University Press, Cambridge, U.K.

PrepLex: a lexicon of French prepositions for parsing

Karën Fort
Calligramme and TALARIS projects
LORIA/INRIA Lorraine / Nancy, France
Karen.Fort@loria.fr

Bruno Guillaume
Calligramme project
LORIA/INRIA Lorraine / Nancy, France
Bruno.Guillaume@loria.fr

Abstract

PrepLex is a lexicon of French prepositions which provides all the syntactic information needed for parsing. It was built by comparing and merging several authoritative lexical sources. This lexicon also includes information about the prepositions or classes of prepositions that appear in French verb subcategorization frames. This resource has been developed as a first step in making current French preposition lexicons available for effective natural language processing.

1 Introduction

When defining lexical entry classes according to categories, an obvious distinction appears between two types of classes. First, the closed classes, comprising elements which can be exhaustively enumerated, for example pronouns or determiners. Second, open classes for which it is impossible to list all the elements (for example, they may vary according to the domain). The four main open classes are nouns, verbs, adjectives and adverbs. The lexicon construction methodology has to be adapted according to the type of class that is being dealt with.

The status of the class of prepositions is difficult to determine. A priori, prepositions may seem to be a closed class, with elements which can be enumerated. In practice, however, a comparison of the different available resources shows that it is not an easy task to exhaustively list prepositions. Besides, they represent more than 14% of French lemma tokens.[1]

A complete lexicon for parsing applications should contain subcategorization information for predicative words (Briscoe and Carroll, 1993; Carroll and Fang, 2004). This subcategorization information often refers to prepositions in the description of their arguments. Arguments are commonly used with a particular preposition (for example *compter sur* [count on]) or a set of semantically linked prepositions (such as *aller* [go] *LOC*, where *LOC* can be any locative preposition).

For deep parsing, we need to distinguish between indirect complements, required by the verb, and adjuncts which do not appear in the verb valence. The following two examples (1a) and (1b) have the same surface structure, in which the two preposition uses for *avec* can only be distinguished semantically: in the first case, it introduces an oblique complement, whereas in the second case, it introduces an adjunct. This issue can be solved using finer-grained semantic information.

1a. *Jean se bat avec Paul*
[Jean fights against Paul]

1b. *Jean se bat avec courage*
[Jean fights with courage]

This distinction leads us to allow two different preposition uses and therefore causes lexical ambiguity. In order to limit this ambiguity, it is important for a lexicon to identify the prepositions which can have both functions (we will call these "argument" prepositions).

[1] see for example, on a newspaper corpus: https://www.kuleuven.be/ilt/blf/rechbaselex_kul.php\#freq (Selva et al., 2002)

Proceedings of the 4th ACL-SIGSEM Workshop on Prepositions, pages 17–24,
Prague, Czech Republic, June 2007.

Our work aims at providing the community with a lexicon that can be directly used by a parser. We focused on syntactic aspects and extended the work to some semantic elements, like semantically linked sets of prepositions (as *LOC*). The generated lexicon is freely available and is expected to be integrated into larger resources for French, whether existing or under development.

Section 2 describes the sources and the comparative methodology we used. Section 3 details the results of the comparison. Section 4 explains how the lexicon was created from the above-mentioned results. Finally, Section 5 shows an example of use of the lexicon in a parsing application.

2 Methodology

In order to use prepositions for parsing, we need a large list, containing both garden-variety prepositions and prepositions that appear in verb subcategorization frames.

2.1 Using syntactic lexicons

Obviously, some lexicons already exist which provide interesting lists of prepositions. This is the case of Le*fff* (Sagot et al., 2006), which contains a long list of prepositions. However, the syntactic part of the lexicon is still under development and it provides only few prepositions in verb subcategorization frames. Besides, some prepositions in Le*fff* are obsolete or rare. The French-UNL dictionary (Sérasset and Boitet, 2000) also contains prepositions, but its coverage is quite limited and the quality of its entries is not homogeneous. Other sources present prepositions in verb subcategorization frames, but the lists are not quite consistent.

We thus collected, as a first step, prepositions from a certain number of resources, lexicons and dictionaries for the garden-variety list, and syntactic lexicons for the argument prepositions list. Two resources belong to both categories, Le*fff* and French-UNL dictionary:

- Le*fff* (Lexique des Formes Fléchies du Français/French inflected form lexicon (Sagot et al., 2006)) is a large coverage (more than 110,000 lemmas) French morphological and syntactic lexicon (see table 1 for an example of a Le*fff* syntactic entry).

  In its latest public version, 2.2.1, Le*fff* contains 48 simple prepositions and 164 multiword prepositions. It also provides information on verb subcategorization frames, which contain 14 argument prepositions.

- UNL (Universal Networking Language (Sérasset and Boitet, 2000)), is a French to disambiguated English dictionary for machine translation, which contains syntactic information in its French part (see table 1 for a UNL example entry).

  UNL has limited coverage (less than 27,000 lemmas), but it provides, in the English part, semantic information that we will consider using in the near future. UNL contains 48 simple prepositions, among which 12 appear in verb subcategorization frames.

2.2 Using reference sources

We then completed the list of prepositions using manually built resources, including lexicons, dictionaries and grammars:

- The Grevisse (Grevisse, 1997) grammar, in its paper version, allowed us to check some intuitions concerning the obsolescence or usage of some prepositions.

- The TLFi (Trésor de la langue française informatisé), that we consulted through the CNRTL[2], and that offers a slightly different list of prepositions. In particular, it contains the forms *voici* and *voilà*, that are seldom quoted in the other available resources.

- Finally, the PrepNet (Saint-Dizier, 2006) prepositions database was used to check the completeness of our list as well as the semantic information provided by other sources.

2.3 Using verb valence dictionaries

We then looked for a way to enrich the list of prepositions appearing in verb subcategorization frames in Le*fff* and UNL, using resources that focus more particularly on verbs:

[2]see: `http://www.cnrtl.fr`

Lefff entry for *dialoguer avec* [to talk to]

```
dialoguer: suj:sn|sinf|scompl,obja:(à-sn|avec-sn),objde:(de-sn|de-scompl|de-sinf)
```

UNL entry for *dialoguer avec* [to talk to]

```
[dialoguer] {AUX(AVOIR),CAT(CATV),GP1(AVEC),VAL1(GN)} "have_talks";
```

DICOVALENCE entry for *dialoguer avec* [to talk to]

```
VAL$       dialoguer: P0 PP<avec>
VTYPE$     predicator simple
VERB$      DIALOGUER/dialoguer
NUM$       29730
EG$        le délégué des étudiants a dialogué avec le directeur de l'école
TR$        spreken, zich onderhouden, een gesprek hebben, onderhandelen
P0$        qui, je, nous, elle, il, ils, on, celui-ci, ceux-ci
PP_PR$     avec
PP$        qui, lui_ton, eux, celui-ci, ceux-ci, l'un l'autre
LCCOMP$    nous dialoguons, je dialogue avec toi
```

SynLex entry for *adapter avec* [to adapt to]

```
adapter    '<suj:sn,obj:sn,obl:avec-sn>'
```

Table 1: Description of some entries with the preposition *avec* [with] in valence dictionaries

- DICOVALENCE, a valence dictionary of French, formerly known as PROTON (van den Eynde and Mertens, 2002), which has been based on the pronominal approach. In version 1.1, this dictionary details the subcategorization frames of more than 3,700 verbs (table 1 gives an example of a DICOVALENCE entry).

  We extracted the simple and multiword prepositions it contains (i.e. more than 40), as well as their associated semantic classes.

- We completed this argument prepositions list with information gathered from SynLex (Gardent et al., 2006), a syntactic lexicon created from the LADL lexicon-grammar tables (Gross, 1975) (see table 1 for a SynLex entry).

Using these sources, we conducted a systematic study of each preposition, checking its presence in each source, whether in verb subcategorization frames or not, as well as its associated semantic class(es). We then grouped the prepositions that appear both as lexical entries and in verb subcategorization frames.

As multiword prepositions show specific characteristics (in particular, their number) and raise particular issues (segmentation), we processed them separately, using the same methodology.

3 Source comparison results

3.1 Simple prepositions

We thus listed 85 simple prepositions, among which 24 appear in verb subcategorization frames (see table 2).

It is noticeable that the different sources use quite different representations of syntactic information as shown in table 1. Le*fff* offers a condensed vision of verbs, in which valence patterns are grouped into one single entry, whereas SynLex uses a flatter representation without disjunction on syntactic categories for argument realization or for optional arguments. To summarize, we could say that DICOVALENCE lies somewhere between Le*fff* and SynLex, since it uses disjunctive representation but has a finer description of syntactic information and hence splits many entries which are collapsed in Le*fff*.

3.2 Multiword prepositions

We obtained a list of 222 multiword prepositions, among which 18 appear in verb subcategorization frames (see table 3). It is to be noticed that only DICOVALENCE and SynLex contain multiword prepositions in verb subcategorization frames. As for Le*fff*, it provides an impressive list of multiword

	Lexicons					Subcategorization frames			
	Le*fff*	TLFi	Grevisse	PrepNet	UNL	Le*fff*	DV[a]	SynLex	UNL
à	X	X	X	loc		319	895 (18 loc)	887 (70 loc)	246
après	X	X	X	loc	X	2	12	1	
aussi					X				
avec	X	X	X	X	X	35	193 (1 loc)	611 (1 loc)	49
chez	X	X	X	loc	X		9 (5 loc)		1
comme	X				X	14	11	10	3
de	X	X	X	deloc	X	310	888 (117 deloc)	1980 (69 deloc)	282
depuis	X	X	X	deloc	X		2	1	
derrière	X	X	X	loc	X		3		
devers	X	X	X						
dixit	X								
emmi		X							
entre	X	X	X	loc	X		19 (3 loc)	4	
hormis	X	X	X	X	X				
jusque	X	X	X		X		7 (7 loc)		
lès	X	X	X						
moyennant	X	X	X	X	X				
par	X	X	X	loc	X	3	38 (4 loc)	73	8
parmi	X	X	X	loc	X		7 (3 loc)	7	
passé		X			X				
selon	X	X	X	X	X		1	1	
voici		X			X				

Table 2: Some simple prepositions in different sources

[a]DICOVALENCE

prepositions (more than 150) which represents an excellent basis for our work.

4 Lexicon construction

The first selection criterion we applied to build the lexicon is that a preposition should appear in at least one source among the above-mentioned ones. Also, we consider a preposition to be an argument preposition if it appears in at least one verb subcategorization frame.

4.1 Manual filtering

We then filtered the prepositions according to very simple criteria. In particular, we identified some prepositions to be removed as they were:

- erroneous, this is the case, for example, of *aussi* (adverb rather than preposition), which is present in the UNL dictionary as a preposition,
- obsolete or very rare, like *emmi* (from TLFi), *devers* (from Le*fff*, TLFi, Grevisse) or *comme de* (from DICOVALENCE).

We also checked the semantic features given in the sources and removed erroneous ones, like *avec* as locative in SynLex and DICOVALENCE.

4.2 Some remarks

Some sources include as prepositions forms that are not universally considered to be prepositions in linguistics. This is the case, in particular, for:

- *comme*, which is not present in the three reference sources (Grevisse, TLFi and PrepNet) as it is ambiguous and can also be used as a conjunction,

	Lexicons					Subcategorization frames			
	Le*fff*	TLFi	Grevisse	PrepNet	UNL	Le*fff*	DV[a]	SynLex	UNL
à cause de	X		X	X					
à la faveur de			X	X					
à partir de	X		X	deloc				1	
afin de	X	X	X	X					
au nord de				loc					
au vu de	X								
auprès de	X	X	X	loc			27 (1 loc)	35	
comme de							1		
conformément à	X			X					
d'avec			X				1	6	
d'entre	X								
en faveur de	X		X	X			13		
face à	X		X				2		
il y a	X								
jusqu'à	X			loc	X		10 (2 loc)		
jusqu'en	X								
jusqu'où	X								
loin de	X		X	loc					
par suite de			X						
pour comble de	X								
près de	X		X	loc					
quant à	X	X	X						
tout au long de	X			X					
vis-à-vis de	X		X	X				1	

Table 3: Some multiword prepositions in different sources

[a]DICOVALENCE

- *il y a* or *y compris*, which only appear in Le*fff*,
- *d'avec*, which only appears in Grevisse and verb subcategorization frames in DICOVALENCE and SynLex.

We decided to keep those forms in the lexicon for practical reasons, keeping the parsing application in mind.

Moreover, even if its coverage is quite large, the created lexicon is obviously not exhaustive. In this respect, some missing entries should be added, namely:

- prepositions from the DAFLES (Selva et al., 2002), like, for example, *au détriment de*,
- prepositions appearing in reference grammars, like *question*, in Grammaire méthodique du français (Riegel et al., 1997),
- some locative prepositions (and, through metonymy, time prepositions) that are prefixed by *jusqu'*, for example *jusqu'auprès de*. This elided form of *jusque* should probably be treated separately, as a preposition modifier. The same goes for *dès*, followed by a time preposition (or a locative one, through metonymy).

However, it is to be noticed that none of these missing prepositions appear in verb subcategorization frames.

This filtering process also allowed us to identify some issues, in particular elisions in multiword forms, like *afin de*, *afin d'*, or contractions like *face à*, *face au* or *à partir de*, *à partir du*, which will be processed in the segmentation step.

Others, like *lès*, which is only used in toponyms in dashed forms (e.g. Bathelémont-lès-Bauzemont), will be processed during named entity segmentation.

4.3 Results

We obtained a list of 49 simple prepositions, of which 23 appear in verb subcategorization frames in at least one source and are therefore considered to be argument prepositions (see table 4).

We also obtain a list of more than 200 multiword prepositions, among which 15 appear in verb subcategorization frames in at least one source and are therefore considered to be argument prepositions (see table 5).

For the time being, we limited the semantic information in the lexicon to *loc* (locative) and *deloc* (source), but we intend to extend those categories to those used in DICOVALENCE (time, quantity, manner). We have already added those to the prepositions database that is being populated.

We also referred to the sources to add the categories of the arguments introduced by argument prepositions.

PrepLex is currently distributed in a text format suitable both for hand-editing and for integration in a parser or other natural language processing tools. In the format we propose, syntactic information is described via feature structures. These feature structures are always recursive structures of depth 2. The external level describes the structure in terms of "arguments" whereas the internal level gives a finer syntactic description of either the `head` or of each argument. This format aims at being modular and at defining some "classes" that share redundant information. In the case of prepositions, the skeleton of the feature structure used by all entries is:

```
Prep : [
head [cat=prep, prep=#, funct=#]
comp [cat=#, cpl=@]
]
```

When instantiated for a particular preposition, 3 feature values are to be provided (written with "#" in the above description) and the last parametrized feature (written with `@`) is optional. When they are in the head sub-structure, features are referred to by their names whereas, in other cases, a prefix notation is used.

```
à [prep=a|LOC; funct=aobj|loc|adj;
   comp.cat=np|sinf; comp.cpl=void|ceque]
après [prep=apres|LOC; funct=obl|loc|adj;
       comp.cat=np]
avec   [prep=avec; funct=obl|adj;
        comp.cat=np]
à_travers [prep=a_travers; funct=obl|adj;
           comp.cat=np]
```

Technically, the only difficult part is to decide how to represent semantic classes of prepositions like *LOC*. Here, we chose to define the whole set of argument prepositions as well as all the semantic classes (noted in uppercase) as possible atomic values for the *prep* feature. We then used the disjunction `a|LOC` to indicate that the preposition *à* can be used, either as a specific preposition or as a locative preposition.

Additionally, we decided to add to the lexicon information about the sources in which the preposition appears, in order to allow filtering for some specific applications. In the case of argument prepositions, we also added information about the preposition's frequency in the source, as well as a relevant example.

We also decided to add corpus-based frequencies to the lexicon. Thus, for each preposition, we provide its frequency per 1000 words, either as found in the DAFLES (Selva et al., 2002), from a newspaper corpus composed of *Le Monde* and *Le Soir* (1998), or as extracted directly from *Le Monde* (1998) with a simple *grep* command, without tagging.

5 Using the lexicon in a NLP system

We briefly expose some parsing problems related to prepositions.

5.1 Segmentation issues

The first issue that appears when integrating prepositions in a parsing system is that of segmentation. In particular, contractions have to be processed specifically so that *au* is identified as the equivalent of *à le*. The same goes for *de*, which can appear in some multiword prepositions and can be elided as *d'*. However, these phenomena are not specific to prepositions. They can be addressed either in the lexicon (for example Le*fff* explicitly contains both

Lexicons						Subcategorization frames				
Le*fff*	TLFi	Grevisse	PrepNet	UNL	**PrepLex**	Le*fff*	DV	SynLex	UNL	**PrepLex**
44	69	55	36	46	**49**	14	24	18	11	**23**

Table 4: Total number of simple prepositions by source

Lexicons						Subcategorization frames				
Le*fff*	TLFi	Grevisse	PrepNet	UNL	**PrepLex**	Le*fff*	DV	SynLex	UNL	**PrepLex**
166	11	77	89	2	**206**	0	16	4	0	**15**

Table 5: Total number of multiword prepositions by source

au cours de and *au cours d'*), or during the segmentation step.

We decided on the second solution as it improves lexicon maintainability.

An issue that is more directly linked to multiword prepositions is that of segmentation ambiguities. For example, in the following two sentences (2a) and (2b) the group of words *au cours de* is a multiword preposition in the first case, but it has to be decomposed in the second one. Other multiword prepositions can never be decomposed, for example *y compris*.

This highlights the fact that segmentation is ambiguous and that it is necessary to be able to keep the segmentation ambiguity through the whole parsing process.

2a. *Il a beaucoup travaillé au cours de cette année*
[He worked hard during the year]

2b. *Il a beaucoup travaillé au cours de M. Durand*
[He worked hard in Mr Durand's course]

5.2 *Adjunct* prepositions vs *argument* prepositions

In deep parsing we have to distinguish between prepositions introducing a verb argument and prepositions introducing adjuncts. However, we have seen that this distinction often relies on semantics and that parsing should leave the two possibilities open. Precise information about argument prepositions and verb subcategorizations eliminates many of these ambiguities.

6 Conclusion

We created a list of French prepositions for parsing applications by comparing various lexicons and dictionaries. We hence focused on syntactic aspects. Manual filtering was used to eliminate obsolete or rare prepositions, as well as a number of errors. The resulting lexicon contains more than 250 French prepositions, among which 49 are simple prepositions.

In syntactic lexicons, subcategorization frames describe prepositions introducing arguments. Prepositions appearing in verbal valence frames are called "argument prepositions". We identified 40 of them.

The produced lexicon is freely available. [3] It will be developed further. In particular, some other information sources will be incorporated. This is the case for the verbs *constructions* fields from the TFLi which contain prepositions, that can be considered as argument prepositions. We plan to use this information to improve the lexicon.

We are also populating a database with this lexical information. [3] This will help us ensure a better maintenance of the lexicon and will allow enrichment of the entries, in particular with examples and associated verbs. We are adding corpus-based frequencies to this database.

A more ambitious task would be to enrich the lexicon with fine-grained semantic information (more detailed than the general classes *loc, deloc, ...*). Many interesting linguistic studies have been conducted on prepositions, including cross-lingual approaches. However, most of them are limited to detailing the semantics of a small number of prepositions; with the exceptions of PrepNet (Saint-Dizier, 2006) for French prepositions and TPP (Litkowski and Hargraves, 2005) (The Preposition Project) for English. It is now necessary to transform those resources in order to make them directly usable by natural language processing systems.

[3] `http://loriatal.loria.fr/Resources.html`

References

Ted Briscoe and John A. Carroll. 1993. Generalized probabilistic LR parsing of natural language (corpora) with unification-based grammars. *Computational Linguistics*, 19(1):25–59.

John A. Carroll and Alex C. Fang. 2004. The automatic acquisition of verb subcategorisations and their impact on the performance of an HPSG parser. In *Proceedings of the 1st International Joint Conference on Natural Language Processing (IJCNLP)*, pages 107–114, Sanya City, China.

Claire Gardent, Bruno Guillaume, Guy Perrier, and Ingrid Falk. 2006. Extraction d'information de sous-catégorisation à partir des tables du LADL. In *Proceedings of TALN 06*, pages 139–148, Leuven.

Maurice Grevisse. 1997. *Le Bon Usage – Grammaire française, édition refondue par André Goosse.* DeBoeck-Duculot, Paris – Leuven, 13th edition.

Maurice Gross. 1975. *Méthodes en syntaxe*. Hermann.

Ken Litkowski and Orin Hargraves. 2005. The preposition project. In *Proc. of the ACL Workshop on Prepositions*.

Martin Riegel, Jean-Christophe Pellat, and René Rioul. 1997. *Grammaire méthodique du français*. PUF, 3rd edition.

Benoit Sagot, Lionel Clément, Éric Villemonte de la Clergerie, and Pierre Boullier. 2006. The Lefff 2 syntactic lexicon for French: architecture, acquisition, use. In *Proc. of LREC 06, Genoa, Italy*.

Patrick Saint-Dizier. 2006. PrepNet: a Multilingual Lexical Description of Prepositions. In *Proc. of LREC 06, Genoa, Italy*, pages 877–885. European Language Resources Association (ELRA).

Thierry Selva, Serge Verlinde, and Jean Binon. 2002. Le DAFLES, un nouveau dictionnaire pour apprenants du français. In *Proc. of EURALEX'2002 (European Association for Lexicography), Copenhagen*.

Gilles Sérasset and Christian Boitet. 2000. On UNL as the future "html of the linguistic content" and the reuse of existing NLP components in UNL-related applications with the example of a UNL-French deconverter. In *Proceedings of COLING 2000, Saarbrücken*.

Karel van den Eynde and Piet Mertens, 2002. *La valence: l'approche pronominale et son application au lexique verbal*, pages 63–104. Cambridge University Press, 13th edition.

Detection of Grammatical Errors Involving Prepositions

Martin Chodorow
Hunter College of CUNY
695 Park Avenue
New York, NY, 10021
mchodoro@hunter.cuny.edu

Joel R. Tetreault and **Na-Rae Han**
Educational Testing Services
Rosedale Road
Princeton, NJ, 08541
jtetreault|nzhan@ets.org

Abstract

This paper presents ongoing work on the detection of preposition errors of non-native speakers of English. Since prepositions account for a substantial proportion of all grammatical errors by ESL (English as a Second Language) learners, developing an NLP application that can reliably detect these types of errors will provide an invaluable learning resource to ESL students. To address this problem, we use a maximum entropy classifier combined with rule-based filters to detect preposition errors in a corpus of student essays. Although our work is preliminary, we achieve a precision of 0.8 with a recall of 0.3.

1 Introduction

The National Clearinghouse for English Language Acquisition (2002) estimates that 9.6% of the students in the US public school population speak a language other than English and have limited English proficiency. Clearly, there is a substantial and increasing need for tools for instruction in English as a Second Language (ESL).

In particular, preposition usage is one of the most difficult aspects of English grammar for non-native speakers to master. Preposition errors account for a significant proportion of all ESL grammar errors. They represented the largest category, about 29%, of all the errors by 53 intermediate to advanced ESL students (Bitchener et al., 2005), and 18% of all errors reported in an intensive analysis of one Japanese writer (Murata and Ishara, 2004). Preposition errors are not only prominent among error types, they are also quite frequent in ESL writing. Dalgish (1985) analyzed the essays of 350 ESL college students representing 15 different native languages and reported that preposition errors were present in 18% of sentences in a sample of text produced by writers from first languages as diverse as Korean, Greek, and Spanish.

The goal of the research described here is to provide software for detecting common grammar and usage errors in the English writing of non-native English speakers. Our work targets errors involving prepositions, specifically those of incorrect preposition selection, such as *arrive <u>to</u> the town*, and those of extraneous prepositions, as in *most <u>of</u> people*.

We present an approach that combines machine learning with rule-based filters to detect preposition errors in a corpus of ESL essays. Even though this is work in progress, we achieve precision of 0.8 with a recall of 0.3. The paper is structured as follows: in the next section, we describe the difficulty in learning English preposition usage; in Section 3, we discuss related work; in Sections 4-7 we discuss our methodology and evaluation.

2 Problem of Preposition Usage

Why are prepositions so difficult to master? Perhaps it is because they perform so many complex roles. In English, prepositions appear in adjuncts, they mark the arguments of predicates, and they combine with other parts of speech to express new meanings.

The choice of preposition in an adjunct is largely constrained by its object (*<u>in</u> the summer*, *<u>on</u> Friday*,

Proceedings of the 4th ACL-SIGSEM Workshop on Prepositions, pages 25–30,
Prague, Czech Republic, June 2007.

at noon) and the intended meaning (*at the beach*, *on the beach*, *near the beach*, *by the beach*). Since adjuncts are optional and tend to be flexible in their position in a sentence, the task facing the learner is quite complex.

Prepositions are also used to mark the arguments of a predicate. Usually, the predicate is expressed by a verb, but sometimes it takes the form of an adjective (*He was fond of beer*), a noun (*They have a thirst for knowledge*), or a nominalization (*The child's removal from the classroom*). The choice of the preposition as an argument marker depends on the type of argument it marks, the word that fills the argument role, the particular word used as the predicate, and whether the predicate is a nominalization. Even with these constraints, there are still variations in the ways in which arguments can be expressed. Levin (1993) catalogs verb alternations such as *They loaded hay on the wagon* vs. *They loaded the wagon with hay*, which show that, depending on the verb, an argument may sometimes be marked by a preposition and sometimes not.

English has hundreds of phrasal verbs, consisting of a verb and a particle (some of which are also prepositions). To complicate matters, phrasal verbs are often used with prepositions (i.e., *give up on someone*; *give in to their demands*). Phrasal verbs are particularly difficult for non-native speakers to master because of their non-compositionality of meaning, which forces the learner to commit them to rote memory.

3 Related Work

If mastering English prepositions is a daunting task for the second language learner, it is even more so for a computer. To our knowledge, only three other groups have attempted to automatically detect errors in preposition usage. Eeg-Olofsson et al. (2003) used 31 handcrafted matching rules to detect extraneous, omitted, and incorrect prepositions in Swedish text written by native speakers of English, Arabic, and Japanese. The rules, which were based on the kinds of errors that were found in a training set of text produced by non-native Swedish writers, targeted spelling errors involving prepositions and some particularly problematic Swedish verbs. In a test of the system, 11 of 40 preposition errors were correctly detected.

Izumi et al. (2003) and (2004) used error-annotated transcripts of Japanese speakers in an interview-based test of spoken English to train a maximum entropy classifier (Ratnaparkhi, 1998) to recognize 13 different types of grammatical and lexical errors, including errors involving prepositions. The classifier relied on lexical and syntactic features. Overall performance for the 13 error types reached 25.1% precision with 7.1% recall on an independent test set of sentences from the same source, but the researchers do not separately report the results for preposition error detection. The approach taken by Izumi and colleagues is most similar to the one we have used, which is described in the next section.

More recently, (Lee and Seneff, 2006) used a language model and stochastic grammar to replace prepositions removed from a dialogue corpus. Even though they reported a precision of 0.88 and recall of 0.78, their evaluation was on a very restricted domain with only a limited number of prepositions, nouns and verbs.

4 The Selection Model

A preposition error can be a case of incorrect preposition selection (*They arrived to the town*), use of a preposition in a context where it is prohibited (*They came to inside*), or failure to use a preposition in a context where it is obligatory (e.g., *He is fond this book*). To detect the first type of error, incorrect selection, we have employed a maximum entropy (ME) model to estimate the probability of each of 34 prepositions, based on the features in their local contexts. The ME Principle says that the best model will satisfy the constraints found in the training, and for those situations not covered in the training, the best model will assume a distribution of maximum entropy. This approach has been shown to perform well in combining heterogeneous forms of evidence, as in word sense disambiguation (Ratnaparkhi, 1998). It also has the desirable property of handling interactions among features without having to rely on the assumption of feature independence, as in a Naive Bayesian model.

Our ME model was trained on 7 million "events" consisting of an outcome (the preposition that appeared in the training text) and its associated context (the set of feature-value pairs that accompanied it). These 7 million prepositions and their contexts were extracted from the MetaMetrics corpus of 1100 and 1200 Lexile text (11th and 12th grade) and newspaper text from the San Jose Mercury News. The sentences were then POS-tagged (Ratnaparkhi, 1998) and then chunked into noun phrases and verb phrases by a heuristic chunker.

The maximum entropy model was trained with 25 contextual features. Some of the features represented the words and tags found at specific locations adjacent to the preposition; others represented the head words and tags of phrases that preceded or followed the preposition. Table 1 shows a subset of the feature list.

Some features had only a few values while others had many. PHR_pre is the "preceding phrase" feature that indicates whether the preposition was preceded by a noun phrase (NP) or a verb phrase (VP). In the example in Table 2, the preposition *into* is preceded by an NP. In a sentence that begins *After the crowd was whipped up into a frenzy of anticipation*, the preposition *into* is preceded by a VP. There were only two feature#value pairs for this feature: PHR_pre#NP and PHR_pre#VP. Other features had hundreds or even thousands of different values because they represented the occurrence of specific words that preceded or followed a preposition. Any feature#value pairs which occurred with very low frequency in the training (less than 10 times in the 7 million contexts) were eliminated to avoid the need for smoothing their probabilities. Lemma forms of words were used as feature values to further reduce the total number and to allow the model to generalize across inflectional variants. Even after incorporating these reductions, the number of values was still very large. As Table 1 indicates, TGR, the word sequence including the preposition and the two words to its right, had 54,906 different values. Summing across all features, the model contained a total of about 388,000 feature#value pairs. Table 2 shows an example of where some of the features are derived from.

5 Evaluation on Grammatical Text

The model was tested on 18,157 preposition contexts extracted from 12 files randomly selected from a portion of 1100 Lexile text (11th grade) that had not been used for training. For each context, the model predicted the probability of each preposition given the contextual representation. The highest probability preposition was then compared to the preposition that had actually been used by the writer. Because the test corpus consisted of published, edited text, we assumed that this material contained few, if any, errors. In this and subsequent tests, the model was used to classify each context as one of 34 classes (prepositions).

Results of the comparison between the classifier and the test set showed that the overall proportion of agreement between the text and the classifier was 0.69. The value of kappa was 0.64. When we examined the errors, we discovered that, frequently, the classifier's most probable preposition (the one it assigned) differed from the second most probable by just a few percentage points. This corresponded to a situation in which two or more prepositions were likely to be found in a given context. Consider the context *They thanked him for his consideration ___ this matter*, where either *of* or *in* could fill the blank. Because the classifier was forced to make a choice in this and other close cases, it incurred a high probability of making an error. To avoid this situation, we re-ran the test allowing the classifier to skip any preposition if its top ranked and second ranked choices differed by less than a specified amount. In other words, we permitted it to respond only when it was confident of its decision. When the difference between the first and second ranked choices was 0.60 or greater, 50% of the cases received no decision, but for the remaining half of the test cases, the proportion of agreement was 0.90 and kappa was 0.88. This suggests that a considerable improvement in performance can be achieved by using a more conservative approach based on a higher confidence level for the classifier.

6 Evaluation on ESL Essays

To evaluate the ME model's suitability for analyzing ungrammatical text, 2,000 preposition contexts were extracted from randomly selected essays written on ESL tests by native speakers of Chinese, Japanese, and Russian. This set of materials was used to look for problems that were likely to arise as a conse-

Feature	**Description**	**No. of values with freq $\geq$ 10**
BGL	Bigram to left; includes preceding word and POS	23,620
BGR	Bigram to right; includes following word and POS	20,495
FH	Headword of the following phrase	19,718
FP	Following phrase	40,778
PHR_pre	Preceding phrase type	2
PN	Preceding noun	18,329
PNMod	Adjective modifying preceding noun	3,267
PNP	Preceding noun phrase	29,334
PPrep	Preceding preposition	60
PV	Preceding verb	5,221
PVP	Preceding verb phrase	23,436
PVtag	POS tag of the preceding verb	24
PVword	Lemma of the preceding verb	5,221
PW	Lemma of the preceding word	2,437
TGL	Trigram to left; includes two preceding words and POS	44,446
TGR	Trigram to right; includes two following words and POS	54,906

Table 1: Some features used in ME Model

<table>
<tr><td>After</td><td><u>whipping</u></td><td>the</td><td><u>crowd</u></td><td>up</td><td>into</td><td>a</td><td><u>frenzy</u></td><td>of</td><td>anticipation...</td></tr>
<tr><td></td><td>PVword</td><td></td><td>PN</td><td>PW</td><td></td><td></td><td>FH</td><td></td><td></td></tr>
<tr><td></td><td></td><td></td><td></td><td>BGL</td><td></td><td>BGR</td><td></td><td></td><td></td></tr>
<tr><td></td><td></td><td></td><td colspan="2">| ——TGL—— |</td><td></td><td colspan="2">| ——TGR—— |</td><td></td><td></td></tr>
</table>

Table 2: Locations of some features in the local context of a preposition

quence of the mismatch between the training corpus (edited, grammatical text) and the testing corpus (ESL essays with errors of various kinds). When the model was used to classify prepositions in the ESL essays, it became obvious, almost immediately, that a number of new performance issues would have to be addressed.

The student essays contained many misspelled words. Because misspellings were not in the training, the model was unable to use the features associated with them (e.g., FHword#frinzy) in its decision making. The tagger was also affected by spelling errors, so to avoid these problems, the classifier was allowed to skip any context that contained misspelled words in positions adjacent to the preposition or in its adjacent phrasal heads. A second problem resulted from punctuation errors in the student writing. This usually took the form of missing commas, as in *I disagree because <u>from</u> my point of view there is no evidence*. In the training corpus, commas generally separated parenthetical expressions, such as *from my point of view*, from the rest of the sentence. Without the comma, the model selected *of* as the most probable preposition following *because*, instead of *from*. A set of heuristics was used to locate common sites of comma errors and skip these contexts.

There were two other common sources of classification error: antonyms and benefactives. The model very often confused prepositions with opposite meanings (like *with/without* and *from/to*), so when the highest probability preposition was an antonym of the one produced by the writer, we blocked the classifier from marking the usage as an error. Benefactive phrases of the form *for + person/organization* (*for everyone, for my school*) were also difficult for the model to learn, most likely because, as adjuncts, they are free to appear in many different places in a sentence and the preposition is not constrained by its object, resulting in their frequency being divided among many different contexts. When a benefactive appeared in an argument position, the model's most probable preposition was generally not the preposition *for*. In the sentence *They described a part <u>for</u> a kid*, the preposition *of* has a higher probability. The classifier was prevented from marking *for + person/organization* as a usage error in such contexts.

To summarize, the classifier consisted of the ME model plus a program that blocked its application

	Rater 1 vs. Rater 2	Classifier vs. Rater 1	Classifier vs. Rater 2
Agreement	0.926	0.942	0.934
Kappa	0.599	0.365	0.291
Precision	N/A	0.778	0.677
Recall	N/A	0.259	0.205

Table 3: Classifer vs. Rater Statistics

in cases of misspelling, likely punctuation errors, antonymous prepositions, and benefactives. Another difference between the training corpus and the testing corpus was that the latter contained grammatical errors. In the sentence, *This was my first experience about choose friends*, there is a verb error immediately following the preposition. Arguably, the preposition is also wrong since the sequence *about choose* is ill-formed. When the classifier marked the preposition as incorrect in an ungrammatical context, it was credited with correctly detecting a preposition error.

Next, the classifier was tested on the set of 2,000 preposition contexts, with the confidence threshold set at 0.9. Each preposition in these essays was judged for correctness of usage by one or two human raters. The judged rate of occurrence of preposition errors was 0.109 for Rater 1 and 0.098 for Rater 2, i.e., about 1 out of every 10 prepositions was judged to be incorrect. The overall proportion of agreement between Rater1 and Rater 2 was 0.926, and kappa was 0.599.

Table 3 (second column) shows the results for the Classifier vs. Rater 1, using Rater 1 as the gold standard. Note that this is not a blind test of the classifier inasmuch as the classifier's confidence threshold was adjusted to maximize performance on this set. The overall proportion of agreement was 0.942, but kappa was only 0.365 due to the high level of agreement expected by chance, as the Classifier used the response category of "correct" more than 97% of the time. We found similar results when comparing the judgements of the Classifier to Rater 2: agreement was high and kappa was low. In addition, for both raters, precision was much higher than recall. As noted earlier, the table does not include the cases that the classifier skipped due to misspelling, antonymous prepositions, and benefactives.

Both precision and recall are low in these comparisons to the human raters. We are particularly concerned about precision because the feedback that students receive from an automated writing analysis system should, above all, avoid false positives, i.e., marking correct usage as incorrect. We tried to improve precision by adding to the system a naive Bayesian classifier that uses the same features found in Table 1. As expected, its performance is not as good as the ME model (e.g., precision = 0.57 and recall = 0.29 compared to Rater 1 as the gold standard), but when the Bayesian classifier was given a veto over the decision of the ME classifier, overall precision did increase substantially (to 0.88), though with a reduction in recall (to 0.16). To address the problem of low recall, we have targeted another type of ESL preposition error: extraneous prepositions.

7 Prepositions in Prohibited Contexts

Our strategy of training the ME classifier on grammatical, edited text precluded detection of extraneous prepositions as these did not appear in the training corpus. Of the 500-600 errors in the ESL test set, 142 were errors of this type. To identify extraneous preposition errors we devised two rule-based filters which were based on analysis of the development set. Both used POS tags and chunking information.

Plural Quantifier Constructions This filter addresses the second most common extraneous preposition error where the writer has added a preposition in the middle of a plural quantifier construction, for example: *some of people*. This filter works by checking if the target word is preceded by a quantifier (such as "some", "few", or "three"), and if the head noun of the quantifier phrase is plural. Then, if there is no determiner in the phrase, the target word is deemed an extraneous preposition error.

Repeated Prepositions These are cases such as *people can find friends with with the same interests* where a preposition occurs twice in a row. Repeated prepositions were easily screened by checking if the same lexical item and POS tag were used for both words.

These filters address two types of extraneous preposition errors, but there are many other types (for example, subcategorization errors, or errors with prepositions inserted incorrectly in the beginning of a sentence initial phrase). Even though these filters cover just one quarter of the 142 extraneous errors, they did improve precision from 0.778 to 0.796, and recall from 0.259 to 0.304 (comparing to Rater 1).

8 Conclusions and Future Work

We have presented a combined machine learning and rule-based approach that detects preposition errors in ESL essays with precision of 0.80 or higher (0.796 with the ME classifier and Extraneous Preposition filters; and 0.88 with the combined ME and Bayesian classifiers). Our work is novel in that we are the first to report specific performance results for a preposition error detector trained and evaluated on general corpora.

While the training for the ME classifier was done on a separate corpus, and it was this classifier that contributed the most to the high precision, it should be noted that some of the filters were tuned on the evaluation corpus. Currently, we are in the course of annotating additional ESL essays for preposition errors in order to obtain a larger-sized test set.

While most NLP systems are a balancing act between precision and recall, the domain of designing grammatical error detection systems is distinguished in its emphasis on high precision over high recall. Essentially, a false positive, i.e., an instance of an error detection system informing a student that a usage is incorrect when in fact it is indeed correct, must be reduced at the expense of a few genuine errors slipping through the system undetected. Given this, we chose to set the threshold for the system so that it ensures high precision which in turn resulted in a recall figure (0.3) that leaves us much room for improvement. Our plans for future system development include:

1. Using more training data. Even a cursory examination of the training corpus reveals that there are many gaps in the data. Seven million seems like a large number of examples, but the selection of prepositions is highly dependent on the presence of other specific words in the context. Many fairly common combinations of Verb+Preposition+Noun or Noun+Preposition+Noun are simply not attested, even in a sizable corpus. Consistent with this, there is a strong correlation between the relative frequency of a preposition and the classifier's ability to predict its occurrence in edited text. That is, prediction is better for prepositions that have many examples in the training set and worse for those with fewer examples. This suggests the need for much more data.

2. Combining classifiers. Our plan is to use the output of the Bayesian model as an input feature for the ME classifier. We also intend to use other classifiers and let them vote.

3. Using semantic information. The ME model in this study contains no semantic information. One way to extend and improve its coverage might be to include features of verbs and their noun arguments from sources such as FrameNet (http://framenet.icsi.berkeley.edu/), which detail the semantics of the frames in which many English words appear.

References

J. Bitchener, S. Young, and D. Cameron. 2005. The effect of different types of corrective feedback on esl student writing. *Journal of Second Language Writing*.

G. Dalgish. 1985. Computer-assisted esl research and courseware development. *Computers and Composition*.

J. Eeg-Olofsson and O. Knuttson. 2003. Automatic grammar checking for second language learners - the use of prepositions. In *Nodalida*.

National Center for Educational Statistics. 2002. Public school student counts, staff, and graduate counts by state: School year 2000-2001.

E. Izumi, K. Uchimoto, T. Saiga, T. Supnithi, and H. Isahara. 2003. Automatic error detection in the japanese leaners' english spoken data. In *ACL*.

E. Izumi, K. Uchimoto, and H. Isahara. 2004. The overview of the sst speech corpus of japanese learner english and evaluation through the experiment on automatic detection of learners' errors. In *LREC*.

J. Lee and S. Seneff. 2006. Automatic grammar correction for second-language learners. In *Interspeech*.

B. Levin. 1993. *English verb classes and alternations: a preliminary investigation*. Univ. of Chicago Press.

M. Murata and H. Ishara. 2004. Three english learner assistance systems using automatic paraphrasing techniques. In *PACLIC 18*.

A. Ratnaparkhi. 1998. *Maximum Entropy Models for natural language ambiguity resolution*. Ph.D. thesis, University of Pennsylvania.

Measuring the Productivity of Determinerless PPs

Florian Dömges, Tibor Kiss, Antje Müller, Claudia Roch
Sprachwissenschaftliches Institut
Ruhr-Universität Bochum

florian.doemges@rub.de
tibor@linguistics.rub.de
antje.mueller@rub.de
claudia.roch@rub.de

Abstract

We determine the productivity of determinerless PPs in German quantitatively, restricting ourselves to the preposition *unter*. The study is based on two German newspaper corpora, comprising some 210 million words. The problematic construction, i.e. *unter* followed by a determinerless singular noun occurs some 16.000 times in the corpus. To clarify the empirical productivity of the construction, we apply a productivity measure developed by Baayen (2001) to the syntactic domain by making use of statistical models suggested in Evert (2004). We compare two different models and suggest a gradient descent search for parameter estimation. Our results show that the combination of *unter*+noun must in fact be characterized as productive, and hence that a syntactic treatment is required.

1 Introduction

The combination of a preposition with a singular count noun, illustrated in (1) with the preposition *unter*, is a frequent construction in written and spoken German. From a theoretical perspective, constructions like (1) are interesting since they seem to violate the near universal rule that determiners should accompany singular count nouns if the language in question shows determiners at all (cf. Himmelmann (1998)).

unter Vorbehalt (with reservation),
unter Androhung (on pain),
unter Lizenz (under licence),
unter Vorwand (pretending) (1)

Baldwin et al. (2006) follow a tradition of English grammar and call constructions like (1) determinerless PPs (D-PP), defined as PPs whose NP-complement consists of a singular count noun without an accompanying determiner (as e.g. English *by bus*, *in mind*). It has been claimed that D-PPs are mostly idiomatic and not productive. Hence, computational grammars often include D-PPs only as stock phrases or listed multiword expressions and do not offer a grammatical treatment. However, both claims have to be doubted seriously. Kiss (2006, 2007) shows that the class of D-PPs does not contain more idiomatic phrases than a typical phrasal category should and also argues against a 'light P hypothesis' which allows a pseudo-compositional treatment of D-PPs by ignoring the semantics of the preposition altogether. Trawinski (2003), Baldwin et al. (2006), as well as Trawinski et al. (2006) offer grammatical treatments of D-PPs, or at least of some subclasses of D-PPs. Interestingly, (Baldwin et al. (2006), 175f.) take the productivity of a subclass of D-PPs for granted and propose a lexical entry for prepositions which select determinerless N's as their complement. While we are sympathetic to a syntactic treatment of D-PPs in a computational grammar, we think that the productivity of such constructions must be considered more closely. The analysis of Baldwin et al. (2006) allows the unlimited combination of prepositions meeting their lexical specification with a determinerless N projection. This

Proceedings of the 4th ACL-SIGSEM Workshop on Prepositions, pages 31–37,
Prague, Czech Republic, June 2007.

assumption is not in line with speaker's intuitions with regard to producing or judging such constructions. As has been pointed out by Kiss (2006, 2007), speakers of German can neither freely produce sequences consisting of *unter* and determinerless N projections (typically a noun) nor can they judge such constructions in isolation. In addition, not even very similar nouns can be interchanged in a D-PP, as can be witnessed by comparing near-synonyms *Voraussetzung* and *Prämisse* which both translate as prerequisite, or as provided in the examples in (2).

The examples in (2) illustrate that *Voraussetzung* cannot be replaced by *Prämisse* in a D-PP (2a, b), while it can be replaced as a head noun in a full PP (2c, d). While the contrast in (2) casts doubt on a productive analysis on the basis of the speakers knowledge of language, the present paper will show that *unter*+noun has to be classified as productive from an empirical perspective.

(2)
a. Auch Philippe Egli besteht auf einer eigenen Handschrift - *unter Voraussetzung* des Einverständnisses des Ensembles.
b. * Auch Philippe Egli besteht auf einer eigenen Handschrift - *unter Prämisse* des Einverständnisses des Ensembles.
c. Auch Philippe Egli besteht auf einer eigenen Handschrift - *unter der Voraussetzung* des Einverständnisses des Ensembles.
d. Auch Philippe Egli besteht auf einer eigenen Handschrift - *unter der Prämisse* des Einverständnisses des Ensembles.

"Philippe Egli insists on his individual way of dealing with the issue, provided the ensemble agrees."

Our investigation is based of a corpus analysis of D-PPs, consisting of the preposition *unter* and a following noun, and employs a quantitative measure of productivity, first developed by Harald Baayen to analyze morphological productivity. The preliminary conclusion to be drawn from this result will be that empirical and intuitive productivity of *unter*+noun sequences do not match.

In applying Baayen's productivity measure to syntactic sequences, however, we are faced with a serious problem. Baayen's productivity measure $P(N)$ is based on the expectation of the hapax legomena – $E[V_1]$ – occurring in a vocabulary of size N, i.e. $P(N) = \frac{E[V_1]}{N}$.

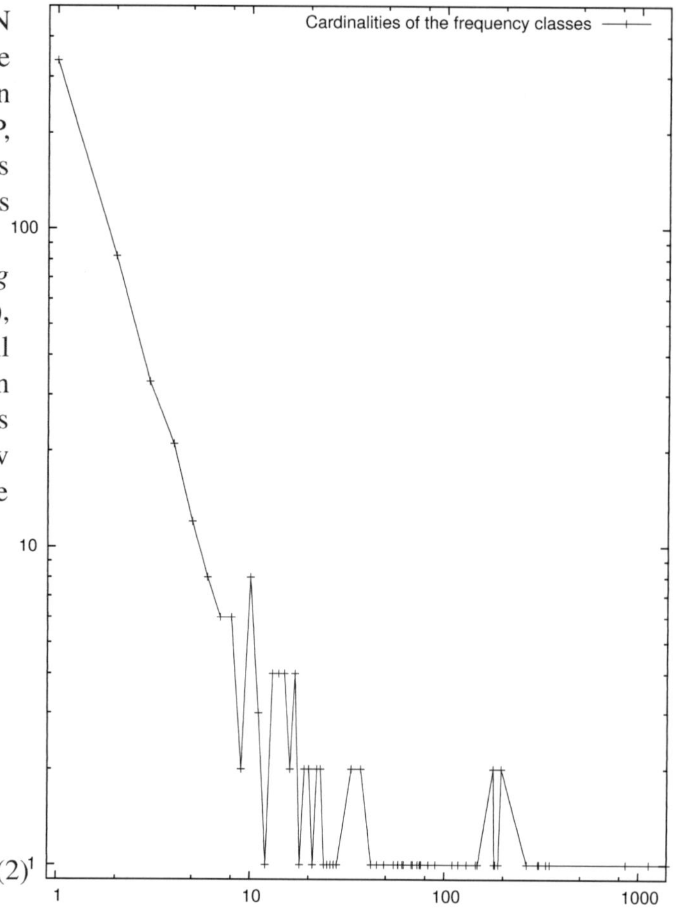

Figure 1: Cardinalities of the frequency classes. The frequency of each type was counted, then the types were grouped into classes of equal frequency. The number of types in each class was counted. The frequency values m are assigned to the x-axis, the size of the class V_m to the y-axis. Both are scaled logarithmically.

Since we cannot derive the expectation of the hapax legomena directly from the corpus, we have to approximate it by use of regression models. To simplify matters somewhat, Baayen's models can only be applied to unigrams, while we have to consider bigrams – the preposition and the adjacent noun. To circumvent this problem, Kiss (2006,2007) calculated $P(N)$ on the basis of the empirical distribution of V_1 as N gets larger. Evert (2004) offers regression models to determine $E[V_1]$ for n-grams and suggests two different models, the Zipf-Mandelbrot model (ZM) and the finite Zipf-Mandelbrot model (fZM). The difference between these two models is that fZM assumes a finite vocabulary. In the present paper, we apply Evert's models to sequences of *unter*+noun. We differ from Evert's proposal in estimating the free parameter α in both models on the basis of the gradient descent algorithm. Contrary to Evert's assumptions, we will show that the results of the ZM model are much closer to the empirical observations than the results of the fZM model.

The paper is structured as follows. Section 2 describes the empirical basis of the experiment, a corpus study of *unter*$+textnoun_{sg}$ sequences. Section 3 introduces the models suggested by Evert (2004). Section 3.1 introduces the models, section 3.2 shows how the free parameter is estimated by making use of the gradient descent algorithm. The results are compared in section 3.3.

2 Corpus Study

The present study is based on two German corpora, with a total of 213 million words: the NZZ-corpus 1995-1998 (Neue Zürcher Zeitung) and the FRR-corpus 1997-1999 (Frankfurter Rundschau). Making use of the orthographic convention that nouns are capitalized in German, we have automatically extracted 12.993 types, amouting to some 71.000 tokens of *unter* and a following noun. From these 12.993 types, we have removed all candidates where the noun is a proper noun, or realized as a plural, or as member of a support verb construction. Also, we have excluded typical stock phrases and all mass nouns. The extraction process was done both manually (proper nouns, mass nouns, support verb constructions) and automatically (plurals, mass nouns).

As a result of the extraction process, a total number of 1.103 types remained, amounting to 16.444 tokens. The frequency of every type was determined and types with the same frequency were grouped into classes. 65 equivalence classes were established according to their frequency m (cf. Figure 1). The number of elements in every class was counted and the various count results were associated with the variables $V_m = V_1, V_2, \ldots, V_{2134}$.

3 LNRE Model Regression

Baayen (2001) uses the term LNRE models (*large number of rare events*) to describe a class of models that allow the determination of the expectation with a small set of parameters. Evert (2004) proposes two LNRE models with are based on Zipf's Law (Zipf(1949), Li (1992)) to identify the expectations $E[V_1], \ldots, E[V_{max}]$. Both models are based on the Zipf-Mandelbrot law.

Zipf's Law (Zipf(1949), Li (1992)) posits that the frequency of the r-most frequent type is proportional to $\frac{1}{r}$. The distribution of random texts displays a strong similarity to the results expected according to Zipf's Law (cp. Li (1992)). Mandelbrot (1962) et al. explain this phenomenon by Zipf's *Principle of Least Effort.*

Rouault (1978) shows that the probability of types with a low frequency asymptotically behaves as posited by the Zipf-Mandelbrot Law

$$\pi_i = \frac{C}{(i+b)^a}$$

with $a > 1$ and $b > 0$.

The models are introduced in section 3.1. Both require a parameter α, whose value was determined by employing a gradient descent algorithm implemented in Perl. The optimal value for the free parameter was found by constructing an error function to minimise α. The calculation was carried out for both models, but better results are produced if the assumption is given up that the vocabulary is finite.

3.1 Finite and general Zipf-Mandelbrot models

Evert (2004) proposes the finite Zipf-Mandelbrot model (fZM) and the general Zipf-Mandelbrot model (ZM) for modelling the expectations of the frequency classes V_m, i.e. $E[V_1], \ldots, E[V_{max}]$ and the expected vocabulary size, i.e. the expectation of the different types $E[V]$. The two models make different assumptions about the probability distributions of the frequency classes. The fZM assumes that there is a minimal probability A – defined as $\exists A : \forall i : A \leq \pi_i$. This amounts to the assumption that the vocabulary size itself is finite. Hence, it can be expected according to the fZM model that the set of observed types does not increase once $N \approx \frac{1}{A}$ is reached. In the general ZM model, there is no such minimal probability.

Assuming a fZM model, Evert (2004) proposes the following results to estimate the expectation of the frequency classes $E[V_m]$ and the expected vocabulary size $E[V]$. In the following equations, B stands for the maximum probability, defined as $\forall i : B \geq \pi_i$.

$$E[V_m] = \frac{1-\alpha}{(B^{1-\alpha} - A^{1-\alpha}) \cdot m!} \cdot$$

$$N^{\alpha} \cdot \Gamma(m - \alpha, N \cdot A) \quad (3)$$

$$E[V] = \frac{1-\alpha}{(B^{1-\alpha} - A^{1-\alpha})} \cdot N^{\alpha} \cdot \frac{\Gamma(1-\alpha, N \cdot A)}{\alpha} +$$

$$\frac{1-\alpha}{(B^{1-\alpha} - A^{1-\alpha}) \cdot \alpha \cdot A^{\alpha}} \cdot (1 - e^{-N \cdot A}) \quad (4)$$

As can be witnessed from the formulae given, N, A, and B are already known or directly derivable from our observations, leaving us with the determination of the free parameter α.

Using the general Zipf-Mandelbrot model, we end with the following estimations, again suggested by Evert (2004):

$$E[V_m] = \frac{1-\alpha}{B^{1-\alpha} \cdot m!} \cdot N^{\alpha} \cdot \Gamma(m - \alpha) \quad (5)$$

$$E[V] = \frac{1-\alpha}{B^{1-\alpha}} \cdot N^{\alpha} \cdot \frac{\Gamma(1-\alpha)}{\alpha} \quad (6)$$

As there is no minimal probability, we are left with the maximal probability B, the token size N, and again a free parameter α.

3.2 Parameter estimation through gradient descent

Since the expectation of the frequency classes in (3) and (5) depend on the free parameter α, this parameter must be estimated in a way that minimises the deviation of expected and observed values. We measure the deviation with a function that takes into account all observed frequencies and their expected values. A function satisfying these criteria can be found by treating observed frequency classes and expectations as real-valued vectors in a vector space.

$$\mathbf{O}^T = (V, V_1, V_2, \ldots, V_{2134}) \in \mathbb{R}^{66} \quad (7)$$

$$\mathbf{E}^T(\alpha) =$$

$$(E(V)(\alpha), E(V_1)(\alpha), \ldots, E(V_{2134})(\alpha)) \in \mathbb{R}^{66} \quad (8)$$

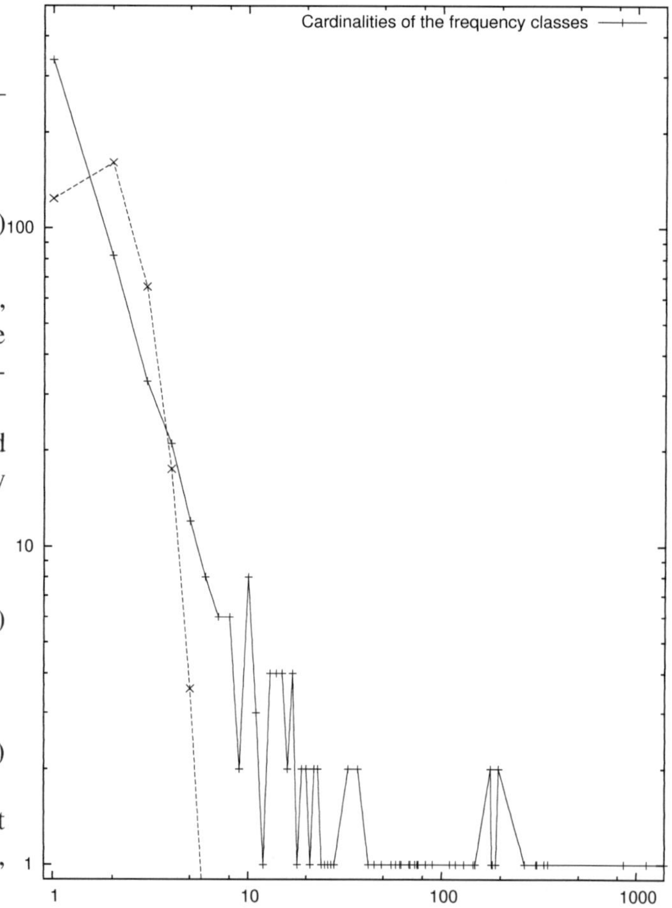

Figure 2: The application of the fZM LNRE Model combined with Rouault's estimation method leads to a strong deviation from the observed data. The observed data is depicted as a solid line, the data from the model as a dotted line. The frequency values m are assigned to the x-axis, the size of the class V_m respectively the expected size $E(V_m)$ to the y-axis. Both are scaled logarithmically.

A natural choice for a measure of error is the quadratic norm of the difference vector between observation and expectation. As we have no information about the relationship between different frequencies we assume that the covariance matrix is the unit matrix.

These thoughts result in the following error function:

$$g(\alpha) = (E(V)(\alpha) - V)^2 +$$

$$\sum_{m=1,\dots,2134} (E(V_m)(\alpha) - V_m)^2 \qquad (9)$$

The minimal α is equal to the root of the derivative of the error function with respect to α. The derivative of the error function is:

$$\frac{\partial g}{\partial \alpha} = 2\frac{\partial E(V)}{\partial \alpha}(E(V)(\alpha) - V) +$$

$$2 \sum_{m=1,\dots,2134} \frac{\partial E(V_m)}{\partial \alpha}(E(V_m)(\alpha) - V_m) \qquad (10)$$

One way to find the minimum $\alpha^* = argmin_\alpha\, g(\alpha)$ would be to derive the expected values with respect to α and solve $g'(\alpha^*) = 0$ for α. As there is no way known to the authors to accomplish this in a symbolic way, the use of a numeric method to calculate α^* is advised.

We chose to find α^* by employing a gradient descent method and approximating $\frac{\partial g}{\partial \alpha}$ by evaluating $g(\alpha)$ in small steps $\epsilon_\alpha(i)$ and calculating $\frac{\Delta g(k)}{\epsilon_\alpha(k)} = \frac{g(\alpha_0+\sum_{j=1}^{k}\epsilon_\alpha(j)) - g(\alpha_0+\sum_{j=1}^{k-1}\epsilon_\alpha(j))}{\epsilon_\alpha(k)}$, where k is number of the iteration.

In the vicinity of a minimum $\frac{\partial g}{\partial \alpha}(\alpha)$ decreases until it vanishes at α^*.

After every iteration the new $\epsilon_\alpha(k)$ is chosen by taking under consideration the change of $\frac{\Delta g(k)}{\epsilon_\alpha(k)}$ and the sign of $\epsilon_\alpha(k-1)$. If $\frac{\Delta g(k)}{\epsilon_\alpha(k)}$ increased, the sign of $\epsilon_\alpha(k-1)$ is inverted: $\epsilon_\alpha(k) = -\epsilon_\alpha(k-1)$.

To prevent the algorithm from oscillating around the minimum the last two values $g(\alpha_0 + \sum_{j=1}^{k-2}\epsilon_\alpha(j))$ and $g(\alpha_0 + \sum_{j=1}^{k-1}\epsilon_\alpha(j))$ are saved.

When a step would result in returning to a previous value $g(\alpha_0 + \sum_{j=1}^{k-1}\epsilon_\alpha(j) + \epsilon_\alpha(k)) = g(\alpha_0 + \sum_{j=1}^{k-2}\epsilon_\alpha(j))$, the step size is multiplied by a constant $0 < \gamma \leq 1$: $\epsilon_\alpha(k) = \gamma\epsilon_\alpha(k-1)$. The algorithm is stopped when the absolute value of the step size drops under a predetermined threshold: $|\epsilon_\alpha(k)| < \epsilon_{threshold}$.

3.3 Results

Interestingly, α as determined by gradient descent on the basis of a fZM leads to a value of 0.666, which does not match well with our observations, as can be witnessed in Figure 2.

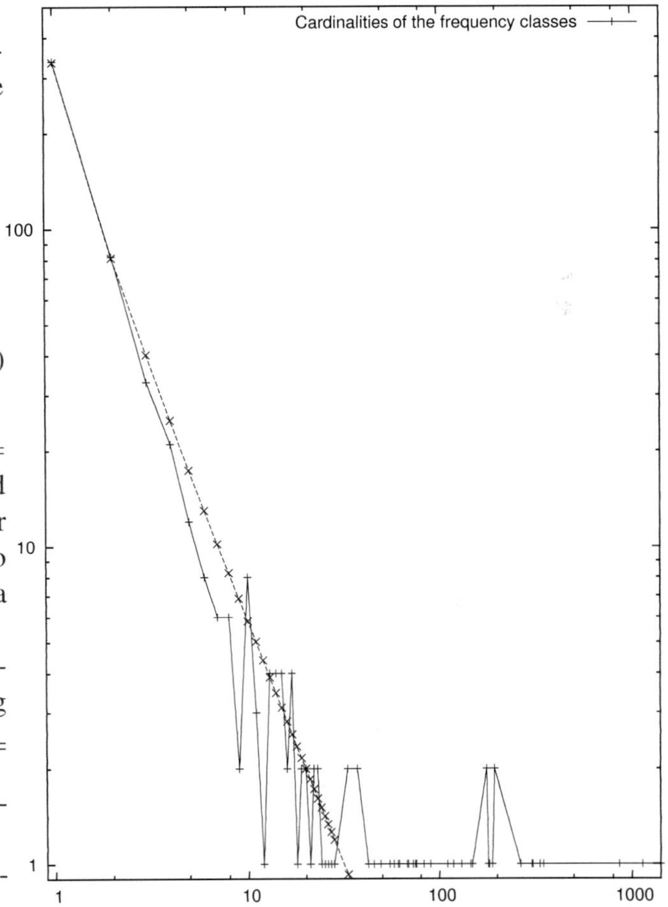

Figure 3: The ZM LNRE Model leads to a far better result with less deviation from the observation. The observed data is depicted as a solid line, the data from the model as a dotted line. The frequency values m are assigned to the x-axis, the size of the class V_m respectively the expected size $E(V_m)$ to the y-axis. Both are scaled logarithmically.

A gradient descent search on the basis of the ZM model delivered a value of $\alpha = 0.515$, a much better approximation (with a χ^2-Value of 4.514), as can be witnessed from Figure 3. The value thus reached also converges with the estimation procedure for α suggested by Rouault (1978), and taken up by Evert (2004), i.e. $\alpha = \frac{V_1}{V}$. Consequently, we assume a ZM model for estimating of expected frequencies.

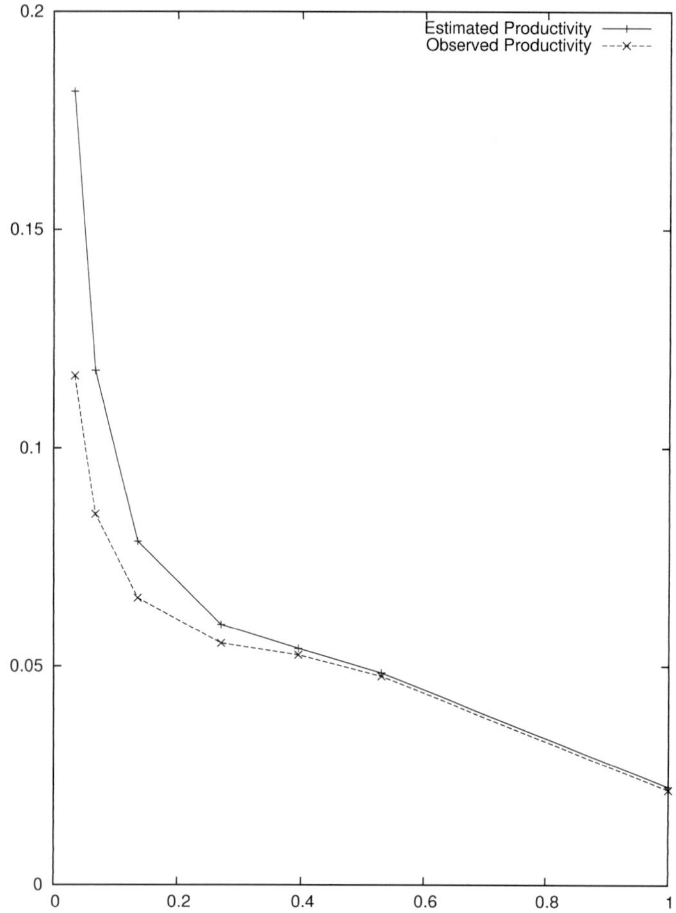

Figure 4: The parts of the corpus were appended to each other and after every step the productivity $P(N)$ was calculated directly from the data as well as from the fitted ZM model. The percentage of the corpus is assigned to the x-axis, the productivity $P(N)$ is assigned to the y-axis. The productivity values that were deduced directly from data are plotted as a dotted line, the productivity values from the ZM model are plotted as a solid line.

To chart the productivity of sequences of the form *unter*+noun, we have divided our corpus into six smaller parts and sampled V, N, and V_1 at these parts. The distribution of the observations thus gained can be found in Figure 4, together with the expectations derived from the ZM model. We observe that both distributions are strikingly similar and converge at the values for the full corpus.

N	V_1	$E[V_1]$	$P(N)$
542	74	96.66	0.182
1068	104	123.47	0.118
2151	169	166.41	0.079
4262	282	249.93	0.059
6222	384	332.19	0.054
8365	469	400.43	0.048
16444	746	748.81	0.022

Table 1: Overview of the observed and expected numbers of hapax legomena and the associated productivity value at different corpus sizes.

In a broader perspective, Figure 4 shows that the combination of *unter*+noun is a productive process, when its empirical distribution is considered. As was already pointed out in section 1, this finding is at odds with speaker's intuitions about combinations of *unter*+noun. Assuming that this result can be extended to other subclasses of D-PPs, we would suggest restricting lexical specifications for prepositions to subclasses of nouns, depending on the pertinent preposition. Future research will have to show whether such clear-cut subclasses can be identified by looking more closely at the empirical findings, other whether we are confronted with a continuum, which would require alternative rule types.

References

Harald Baayen. 2001. *Word Frequency Distributions.* Kluwer, Dordrecht.

Timothy Baldwin, John Beavers, Leonoor van der Beek, Francis Bond, Dan Flickinger, and Ivan A. Sag. 2006. *In Search of a Systematic Treatment of Determinerless PPs.* In Patrick Saint-Dizier, editor, *Syntax and Semantics of Prepositions*, pages 163–179. Springer.

Stefan Evert. 2004. *A Simple LNRE Model for Random Character Sequences.* In *Proceedings of the 7mes Journees Internationales d'Analyse Statistique des Donnees Textuelles*, pages 411–422.

Nikolaus Himmelmann. 1998. *Regularity in Irregularity: Article Use in Adpositional Phrases. Linguistic Typology*, 2:315–353.

Tibor Kiss. 2006. *Do we need a grammar of irregular sequences?* In Miriam Butt, editor, *Proceedings of KONVENS*, pages 64–70, Konstanz.

Tibor Kiss. 2007. *Produktivität und Idiomatizität von Präposition-Substantiv-Sequenzen. forthcoming in Zeitschrift für Sprachwissenschaft.*

W. Li. 1992. *Random texts exhibit zipf's-law-like word frequency distribution. IEEE Transactions on Information Theory.*

B. Mandelbrot. 1962. *On the theory of word frequencies and on related Markovian models of discourse. American Mathematical Society.*

A. Rouault. 1978. *Lois de Zipf et sources markoviennes. Annales de l'Institut H. Poincare.*

Beata Trawinski, Manfred Sailer, and Jan-Philipp Soehn. 2006. *Combinatorial Aspects of Collocational Prepositional Phrases.* In Patrick Saint-Dizier, editor, *Syntax and Semantics of Prepositions*, pages 181–196. Springer.

Beata Trawinski. 2003. *The Syntax of Complex Prepositions in German: An HPSG Approach.* In *Proceedings of GLIP*, volume 5, pages 155–166.

G. K. Zipf. 1949. *Human Behavior and the Principle of Least Effort.* Addison-Wesley, Campridge.

Inferring the semantics of temporal prepositions in Italian

Tommaso Caselli **Valeria Quochi**

ILC-CNR
Via Moruzzi, 1 56123, Pisa, Italy
Dip. Linguistica "T.Bolelli", Università degli Studi di Pisa
Via S.ta Maria, 36, 56100, Pisa, Italy
tommaso.caselli,valeria.quochi@ilc.cnr.it

Abstract

In this work we report on the results of a preliminary corpus study of Italian on the semantics of temporal prepositions, which is part of a wider project on the automatic recognition of temporal relations. The corpus data collected supports our hypothesis that each temporal preposition can be associated with one prototypical temporal relation, and that deviations from the prototype can be explained as determined by the occurrence of different semantic patterns. The motivation behind this approach is to improve methods for temporal annotation of texts for content based access to information. The corpus study described in this paper led to the development of a preliminary set of heuristics for automatic annotation of temporal relations in text/discourse.

1 Introduction

In this work we report on the preliminary results of a corpus study, of contemporary Italian, on temporal relations that hold between a temporal adjunct and an event as a way to determine the semantics of temporal prepositions. We claim, following Schilder and Habel (2001), that the semantics of temporal prepositions is *rel (e, t)*, where *rel* is used to indicate the temporal relation associated with a certain preposition, *t* represents the meaning of the Temporal Expression (timex), and *e* the meaning of the event description involved.

Prepositions introducing a temporal adjunct are explicit signals of temporal relations. The ability to determine temporal relations between timexes introduced by prepositions and events is fundamental for several NLP tasks like Open-Domain Question-Answering systems (Hartrumpf et al. 2006, and Pustejovsky et al. 2002) and for Textual Entailment and Reasoning.

The corpus data collected seems to support our hypothesis that each temporal preposition can be associated with one prototypical temporal relation, and that deviations from the prototype can be explained as determined the occurrences of different semantic pattern.

The work described in this paper is part of a larger project we are conducting on temporal discourse processing in Italian, as proposed in Mani and Pustejovsky (2004).

2 Background

This section presents a brief overview of the TimeML specification language (Pustejovsky et al. 2005), which has been used as the starting point for this work, and some theoretical issues on Italian prepositions.

2.1 TimeML

The TimeML specification language (Pustejovsky et al. 2005) offers a guideline for annotation of timexes, events and their relations. Like other annotation schemes[1], TimeML keeps separated temporal expressions and events, tagged, respectively, with **TIMEX3** and **EVENT**. In addition, two other tags are used: **SIGNAL** and **LINK**.

The **EVENT** tag is used to annotate events, defined as something which occur or happen, and

[1] Filatova and Hovy (2001), Schilder and Habel (2001), Setzer (2001).

Proceedings of the 4th ACL-SIGSEM Workshop on Prepositions, pages 38–44,
Prague, Czech Republic, June 2007.

states, defined as situations in which something holds true.

Temporal expressions, or timexes, like day times (*noon, the evening, 1p.m…*), dates of different granularity (*yesterday, February 2 2007, last week, last spring, last centuries…*), durations (*five hours, in recent years…*) and sets (*twice a day…*), are annotated with the **TIMEX3** tag. This tag is based on specifications given by Ferro et al. (2001) and Setzer (2001). Each timex is assigned to one of the following types: DATE, for calendar times, TIME, for times of the day, even if indefinites (e.g. 'the evening'), DURATION, for timexes expressing a duration, and SET, for sets of times. Each timex is further assigned a value, according to the ISO 8601 specifications (for instance, *3 anni* '3 years' is normalized as "P3Y", i.e. a "period of 3 years").

Function words which explicitly signal a relation between two elements (timex and event, timex and timex, or event and event) are tagged with **SIGNAL**.

Finally, the **LINK** tag is used to specify the relation between two entities. It may indicate a temporal relation (**TLINK**), a subordinating relation (**SLINK**) or an aspectual relation (**ALINK**). The **TLINK** tag, which is pivotal for the present work, comprises 15 relations, only 13 of which are purely temporal. The 13 relations can be seen as derived from Allen's (1984) temporal logic, and 6 of them are binary relations - one being the inverse of the other. These relations (`simultaneous`, `includes`, `is_included`, `during`, `inv_during`, `begin`, `end`, `begun_by`, `ended_by`, `before`, `after`) make explicit the temporal relation holding between two elements.

2.2 Temporal PPs in Italian

Italian prepositions can be divided into two main groups: monosyllabic like *a*, *da*, *in*, *per*, *tra*, -and polysyllabic ones like *fino a* 'up to', *dopo* 'after',, *prima* 'before'…This difference at a surface level reflects a difference also at a semantic level: monosyllabic prepositions are either semantically empty elements (i.e. when they are particles preselected by the VP), or they bear a very abstract relational meaning, which gets specialized on the basis of the co-text; polysyllabic prepositions, on the other hand, have a more specific meaning of their own. For instance, the preposition *dopo* 'after' always means "subsequently, afterwards", disregarding its co-text; which makes the identification of the relation between the elements involved an easier task. In addition to this, most prepositions, both polysyllabic and monosyllabic, belong to different semantic fields, e.g. spatial, temporal, manner or other.

For the purpose of this work, any preposition followed by a timex, as defined in TimeML (Section 2.1), is considered a temporal preposition. Consequently, we will speak of Temporal PP for any sequence of the form "preposition + timex".

In Italian, as in many other languages, the form that Temporal PPs, or temporal adjuncts, may take is influenced by the aspect and actionality of the VP. In traditional grammars, for instance, it is claimed that they can be introduced by *in* if the lexical aspect denotes a telic event (e.g. (1)) and by *per* if the lexical aspect denotes a process or a particular subclass of telic events, i.e. achievements (e.g. (2)). Moreover, these kinds of Temporal PPs necessarily refer to the conclusion of the process denoted by the events and thus are incompatible with the progressive aspect:

1) *a.* Maria ha pulito la stanza *in mezz'ora.*
   [Maria cleaned the room in half an hour]
   b. La pizza arriva *in cinque minuti.*
   [The pizza will arrive in five minutes]
2) *a.* Marco ha lavorato *per due ore.*
   [Marco has worked for two hours]
   b. Marco mi prestò il libro *per due giorni.*
   [Marco lend me his book for two days]

The influence of the aspect and actionality of the VP has an impact also in the identification of their meaning. In particular, in example 1) *a.* the preposition signals that the event of cleaning the room lasted for half an hour, while in the example 1) *b.* the event of arriving takes place after five minutes from the utterance time. In example 1), thus, the same Temporal PP, i.e. IN + timex, has two different meanings, signalled by the relations `includes` and `after`. The different temporal relations are determined by two different semantic patterns: [DURATIVE_Verb] + *in* + [TIMEX type: DURATION] for 1) *a*, and [TELIC_Verb] + *in* + [TIMEX type: DURATION], for 1) *b*.

3 The corpus study

In order to verify our hypothesis that the most frequent temporal relations represents the prototypical meaning of a temporal preposition[2], a corpus study has been conducted. It is important to note that we do not refer to frequency *tout court*, but is frequency with respect to a certain semantic pattern. Since we want to develop a system for automatic annotation of temporal relations, a 5 million word syntactically shallow parsed corpus of contemporary Italian, drawn from the PAROLE corpus, has been used[3].

All occurrences of a prepositional chunk with their left contexts has then been automatically extracted and imported into a database structure using a dedicated *chunkanalyser* tool[4]. This automatically generated DB was then augmented with ontological information from the SIMPLE Ontology, by associating the head noun of each prepositional chunk to its ontological type, and has been queried in order to extract all instances of Temporal PPs, by restricting the nouns headed by prepositions to the type "TIME", which is defined in SIMPLE as "all nouns referring to temporal expressions" (SIMPLE Deliverable 2.1: 245).

To identify the meaning of temporal prepositions, therefore, we considered sequences of the form:

Fin Vb Chunk + Prep Chunk: semtype= TIME

where *Fin Vb Chunk* is a shallow syntactic constituent headed by a finite verb and corresponds to the "anchoring" event, and *Prep Chunk* is the prepositional phrase that represents an instance of a timex. To get a more complete picture of the distribution of Temporal PPs in text, we extracted sequences from zero up to a maximum of two intervening chunks, obtaining a set of about 14,000 such sequences.

A first observation is about the distribution of the Temporal PPs. As illustrated in Table 1 (below) Temporal PPs tend to occur immediately after the event they are linked to.

Sequence	Distance	# Occurrences
Fin_Vb + PP (Time)	0	5859
Fin_Vb + PP (Time)	1	4592
Fin_Vb + PP (Time)	2	3677

Table 1. Occurrences of Temporal PPs with respect to the distance from the event.

The data in Table 1 show that Temporal PPs have a behavior similar to modifiers, like adjectives anchoring on the time axis of the event they refer to.

3.1 Annotating Temporal Relations

To identify the semantics of temporal prepositions, a subcorpus of 1057 sequences of *Fin Vb Chunk + Prep Chunks (Time)* was manually annotated by one investigator with temporal relations in a bottom-up approach.

The tags used for the temporal relation annotation were taken from the TimeML **TLINK** values (see Section 2.1). This will restrict the set of possible relations to a finite set. To ease the task, we excluded the inverse relations for `includes`, `during`, `begin`, and `end`. In order to understand the role of the co-text, we also marked the types of timexes according to the TimeML **TIMEX3** tag (ibid.). In this annotation experiment we did not consider information from the VP because it will be relevant to explain the deviations from the prototype.

. To facilitate the assignment of the right temporal relation, we have used paraphrase tests. All the paraphrases used have the same scheme, based on the formula *rel (e, t)*, illustrated in the 3):

3) *The event/state of X is R timex.*

where X stands for the event identified by the *Fin Vb Chunk*, R is the set of temporal relations and timex is the temporal expression of the Temporal PP. This means that the sequence in 4):

4) [[$_{\mathrm{Vfin}}$[Sono stato sposato] [[$_{\mathrm{PP}}$[*per* quatto anni]]
'I have been married for four years'

can be paraphrased as 5):

5) The state of "being married" happened *during* four years.

[2] We assume and extend Haspelmath's (forth.) proposal on the explanatory and predictive power of frequency of use.
[3] The corpus was parsed with the CHUNK-IT shallow parser (Lenci et al. 2003).
[4] By courtesy of Ing. E. Chiavaccini.

The only temporal relation that is not paraphrased in this way is `simultaneous`, which corresponds to 6):

6) *The event/state X HAPPENS(-ED) AT timex.*

4 Results

Among the 1057 sequences in our sub-corpus, we found that only 37.46% (for a total of 449 excerpts) where real of instances of Temporal PPs, the others being either false positives or complex timexes, i.e. timexes realized by a sequence of a NP followed by a PP introduced by "*di*" (of), as in the following example:

7) [$_{NP}$[la notte]] [$_{PP}$[di Natale]
'the Christmas night'

In Table 2 (below) we report the temporal prepositions identified in the corpus:

Temporal Preposition	# occurrences
In 'in'	91
A 'at/on'	64
Da 'from/since/for'	37
Dopo 'after'	1
Attraverso 'through'	1
Di 'of'	43
Durante 'during'	5
Entro 'by'	9
Fino a 'up to'	6
Fino da 'since'	3
Oltre 'beyond'	1
Per 'for'	50
Tra 'in'	3
Verso 'towards'	1

Table 2. Instances of temporal prepositions in the corpus.

The relative low number of real Temporal PPs can negatively influence the analysis and the identification of the semantics of the temporal prepositions. In order to verify whether the data collected could represent a solid and consistent baseline for further analysis, we analysed all instances of false positive timexes. With the exception of a few cases, which could have been easily recognized by means of a Timex Grammar, we found out that 482/608 instances are represented by nouns which have some sort of temporal value but whose assignment to the semantic type "Time" in the Ontology do not correspond to the given definition (Section 3), e.g: *colazione* 'breakfast', *scuola* 'school', *presidenza* 'presidency', and many others.

Therefore, we performed a new extraction of sequences excluding all instances of false positives. The new results are very different since more than 56.03% of all prepositional chunks are Temporal PPs. This provides support to the fact that the sequences extracted from the sub-corpus, though small in number, can be considered as a consistent starting point for identifying the semantics of temporal prepositions. In particular, the prepositions presented in Table 2 correspond to the most frequent prepositions which give rise to temporal relations between timexes and events. Though small, the 449 sequences prove to be reliable: we have identified a total of 320 temporal relations, as illustrated in Table 3:

Temporal Relation	# occurrences
Includes	87
During	72
Before	11
After	11
Imm_before	1
Imm_after	2
Simultaneous	5
Beginning	52
Ending	10
No Temporal Link	60
No Assigned	9

Table 3. Kinds of Temporal Relation Identified.

5 Inferring Preposition Semantics

The analysis we propose for each single preposition provides information on its semantics. Such information is obtained on the basis of the frequency[5] with which a given temporal relation is associated or coded by that preposition. We claim, as already stated, that temporal relations coded by prepositions are signals of a certain semantic pattern. Different temporal relations coded by the same preposition signal different semantic pattern. According to the frequency with which a temporal relation, or a semantic pattern, occurs, it is considered either as the prototypical (i.e. most frequent) meaning or as a deviation from the norm, whose

[5] Note that what counts is relative frequencies, and not absolute frequencies.

explanation relies in the analysis of the semantic pattern in which it occurs. It is for this reason that a major role in this analysis is played by the types of timexes which follow the preposition. Keeping track of their types, according to the TimeML classification (Section 2.1), is very useful mainly for cases where the same temporal preposition codes different temporal relations depending on the type of the timex by which it is followed. In other words, it is a way to assess the semantic pattern which has been used to code that meaning. In the following sections we will focus on the semantics of the most frequent temporal prepositions, that is *in* 'in', *a* 'at, on', *per* 'for'[6], *da* 'for, since, from'. Cases of low frequency temporal relations are not analyzed here because they would require both more data and a separate investigation.

5.1 Prepositions *per* and *da*

These two prepositions, although they encode different temporal relations, are presented in a unique subsection due to their extremely similar coherent distribution across temporal relations. In particular, the 80% (40/50) of *per* identifies a DURING temporal relation, and 83.78% (31/37) of *da* identifies a BEGIN temporal relation.

From these data, we can represent the semantics of *per* as follows:

8) λ(e, λ(t, DURING (e, t))

and that of *da* as:

9) λ(e, λ(t, BEGIN (e,t))

5.2 The Preposition *in*

The preposition *in* is by far the most used temporal preposition. In our corpus there are 91 occurrences of this preposition, distributed as follows:

INCLUDES (57/91: 62.63%)
DURING (19/91: 20.87%)
AFTER (6/91: 6.59%)
BEGIN (3/91: 3.29%)
SIMULTANEOUS (2/91: 2.19%)
No LINK (2/91: 2.19%)
END (1/91: 1.09%)

Following our idea that the most frequent relation represents the prototypical meaning of the preposition; we claim that Temporal PPs introduced by *in* tend to code a relation of inclusion, semantically represented as:

10) λ(e, λ(t, INCLUDES(e, t)).

Since this preposition is not exclusively used with this meaning, the data forces us to provide an explanation for the other relations identified, in particular for DURING, AFTER and BEGIN.

Considering the DURING relation, we analyzed the types of timexes governed by the preposition but found that type distinctions did not help. Nevertheless, we observed a clearcut regularity analysing the normalized values of the timexes involved: we found that, whenever the timexes are definite quantified intervals of time (e.g. *2 days, 3 years, half an hour*) or temporally anchored instants, *in* encodes the temporal relation of DURING, thus deviating from the default interpretation represented in 10).

The relation AFTER shares with DURING the restriction on the normalized values of the timexes. However, for the AFTER relation there is a strong contribution from the VP, as claimed in traditional grammars. In such cases, it is the actionality of the VP that forces the interpretation of *in* to express the AFTER relation. In fact, this relation appears to occur only with achievement verbs, which inherently focus on the *telos* – or ending point (see example 1) *b* Section 1).

Finally, the BEGIN relation can be found only with aspectual verbs, e.g. *iniziare* 'begin' or *riprendere* 'resume'. In these cases the preposition does not really work as a temporal preposition, but more as a particle selected by the verb.

5.3 The Preposition *a*

The preposition *a* presents a non-trivial distribution, which makes it difficult to identify a prototypical value:

INCLUDES (20/64: 31.25%)
No LINK (19/64: 29.68%)
BEGINS (7/64: 10.93%)
ENDS (4/64: 6.25%)
SIMULTANEOUS (2/64: 3.12%)

---

[6]Note that the Italian preposition "*per*" corresponds only to a subset of uses of the English preposition "for" as in the example:

a) Suonò *per* un'ora [She played *for* an hour.]

However, with NoLINK relations the preposition *a* does not have a temporal value, rather it is used to express either quantities of time (and it usually corresponds to "how many times an event occurs or happens") or it can be considered as a particle selected by the VP. Therefore, if we exclude the NoLINK relations, we can consider that a Temporal PP introduced by *a* typically expresses a relation of inclusion. Further support to this observation can be observed in the possibility of substituting *a* with *in*, at least in the temporal domain. The semantics of the preposition is the following:

11) `λ(e, λ(t, INCLUDES(e, t)).`

As for the BEGINS and ENDS relations, the behaviour is the same as for the preposition *in*, i.e. they are activated by aspectual verbs.

6 Conclusion and Future Work

In this preliminary study we showed that prepositions heading a Temporal PP can be associated with one default temporal relation and that deviations from the norm are due to co-textual influences. The prototypical semantics of temporal prepositions can be represented as in 8)-11).

We also showed that the normalized values of timexes play a major role in the identification of temporal preposition semantics, more than the bare identification of their types. Instances of deviations from the prototypical meaning which could not be explained by differences in the timexes forced us to analyse the VPs, thus providing useful information for the definition of the heuristics.

An important result of this work is the definition of a preliminary set of heuristics for automatic annotation of temporal relations in text/discourse. Our study also suggests a possible refinement of the SIMPLE Ontology aimed at its usability for temporal relation identification; and it can be seen as a starting point for the development of a Timex Grammar.

In the next future we intend to implement this set of heuristics with a machine learning algorithm to evaluate their reliability. All wrongly annotated relations could be used for the identification of the relevant information to determine the contribution of the VP.

Some issues are still open and need further research, in particular it will be necessary to investigate the role of some 'complex' Temporal PPs (e.g. *in questo momento* 'in this moment', which can be paraphrased as 'now'), and how to extract the meaning of Temporal PPs as suggested in Schilder (2004).

References

Allen F. James. 1984. Towards a General Theory of Action and Time. *Artificial Intelligence*, (23):123-54

Ferro Lisa, Mani Inderjeet, Sundheim Beth and Wilson George. 2001. *TIDES Temporal Annotation Guidelines: Version 1.0.2.* MITRE Technical Report, MTR 01W0000041

Filatova, Elena and Hovy, Eduard. 2001. Assigning Time-Stamps To Event –Clauses. *Proceedings of the ACL Workshop on Temporal and Spatial Information, Toulouse, France, 6-1 July*, pages 88-95

Haspelmath, Martin. 2007 (forthcoming). Frequency vs. iconicity in explaining grammatical asymmetries (ms).

Lassen Tine. 2006. An Ontology-Based View on Prepositional Senses. *Proceedings of the Third ACL-SIGSEM Workshop on Prepositions* pages 45-50.

Lenci Alessandro, Montemagni Simonetta and Vito Pirrelli. 2003. CHUNK-IT. An Italian Shallow Parser for Robust Syntactic Annotation, in *Linguistica Computazionale* (16-17).

Mani Inderjeet and James Pustejovsky. 2004. Temporal Discourse Models for Narrative Structure. *ACL Workspoh on Discourse Annotation*

Hartrumpf Sven, Helbig Hermann and Rainer Osswald. 2006. Semantic Interpretation of Prepositions for NLP Applications. *Proceedings of the Third ACL-SIGSEM Workshop on Prepositions*, pages 29-36.

Pustejovky James, Belanger Louis, Castaño José, Gaizauskas Robert, Hanks Paul, Ingria Bob, Katz Graham, Radev Dragomir, Rumshisky Anna, Sanfilippo Antonio, Sauri Roser, Setzer Andrea, Sundheim Beth and Marc Verhagen, 2002. *NRRC Summer Workshop on Temporal and Event Recognition for QA Systems.*

Pustejovsky James, Ingria Robert, Saurí Roser, Castaño José, Littman Jessica, Gaizauskas Robert, Setzer Andrea, Katz Graham and Inderjeet Mani. 2005. The Specification Language TimeML. *The Language of Time: A Reader*, Mani Inderjeet, Pustejovsky james and Robert Gaizauskas (eds), OUP.

Ruimy N., et al. 1998. The European LE-PAROLE Project: The Italian Syntactic Lexicon. *Proceedings of the LREC1998*, Granada, Spain.

Saint-Dizier Patrick.2006. *Syntax and Semantics of Prepositions,* (ed.), Springer, Dordrecht, The Netherlands.

Schilder Frank and Habel Christopher. 2001. Semantic Tagging Of News Messages. *Processing of the ACL Workshop on Temporal and Spatial Information, Toulouse, France, 6-1 July*, pages 65-72

Schilder Frank. 2004 Extracting meaning fron Temporal Nouns and Temporal Prepositions. *ACM Transactions on Asian Language Information Processing*, (3) 1:33-50

Setzer Andrea. 2001. *Temporal Information in Newswire Article: an Annotation Scheme and Corpus Study*, Ph.D. Thesis, University of Sheffield.

SIMPLE Work Package D2.1, available at < http://www.ub.es/gilcub/SIMPLE/simple.html>.

Van Eynde Frank. 2006. On the prepositions which introduce an adjunct of duration. *Proceedings of the Third ACL-SIGSEM Workshop on Prepositions* pages 73-80.

Automatically acquiring models of preposition use

Rachele De Felice and Stephen G. Pulman
Oxford University Computing Laboratory
Wolfson Building, Parks Road, Oxford OX1 3QD, UK
{rachele.defelice|stephen.pulman}@comlab.ox.ac.uk

Abstract

This paper proposes a machine-learning based approach to predict accurately, given a syntactic and semantic context, which preposition is most likely to occur in that context. Each occurrence of a preposition in an English corpus has its context represented by a vector containing 307 features. The vectors are processed by a voted perceptron algorithm to learn associations between contexts and prepositions. In preliminary tests, we can associate contexts and prepositions with a success rate of up to 84.5%.

1 Introduction

Prepositions have recently become the focus of much attention in the natural language processing community, as evidenced for example by the ACL workshops, a dedicated Sem-Eval task, and The Preposition Project (TPP, Litkowski and Hargraves 2005). This is because prepositions play a key role in determining the meaning of a phrase or sentence, and their correct interpretation is crucial for many NLP applications: AI entities which require spatial awareness, natural language generation (e.g. for automatic summarisation, QA, MT, to avoid generating sentences such as **I study at England*), automatic error detection, especially for non-native English speakers. We present here an approach to learning which preposition is most appropriate in a given context by representing the context as a vector populated by features referring to its syntactic and semantic characteristics. Preliminary tests on five prepositions - *in, of, on, to, with* - yield a success rate of between 71% and 84.5%. In Section 2, we illustrate our motivations for using a vector-based approach. Section 3 describes the vector creation, and Section 4 the learning procedure. Section 5 presents a discussion of some preliminary results, and Section 6 offers an assessment of our method.

2 Contextual features

Modelling preposition use is challenging because it is often difficult to explain why in two similar contexts a given preposition is correct in one but not the other. For example, we say A is *similar **to** B*, but *different **from** C*, or we *study **in** England*, but ***at** King's College*. Nor can we rely on co-occurrence with particular parts of speech (POS), as most prepositions have a reasonably wide distribution. Despite this apparently idiosyncratic behaviour, we believe that prepositional choice is governed by a combination of several syntactic and semantic features. Contexts of occurrence can be represented by vectors; a machine learning algorithm trained on them can predict with some confidence, given a new occurrence of a context vector, whether a certain preposition is appropriate in that context or not.

We consider the following macro-categories of features to be relevant: POS being modified; POS of the preposition's complement; given a RASP-style grammatical relation output (GR; see e.g. Briscoe et al. 2006), what GRs the preposition occurs in; named entity (NE) information - whether the modified or complement items are NEs; WordNet information - to which of the WordNet lexicographer

Proceedings of the 4th ACL-SIGSEM Workshop on Prepositions, pages 45–50,
Prague, Czech Republic, June 2007.

classes[1] the modified and complement nouns and verbs belong; immediate context - POS tags of ± 2 word window around the preposition. For example, given a sentence such as *John drove **to** Cambridge*, we would note that this occurrence of the preposition ***to*** modifies a verb, its complement is a location NE noun, the verb it modifies is a 'verb of motion', the tags surrounding it are NNP, VBD, NNP[2], and it occurs in the relation 'iobj' with the verb, and 'dobj' with the complement noun.

Our 307-feature set aims to capture all the salient elements of a sentence which we believe could be involved in governing preposition choice, and which can be accurately recognised automatically. Our choice of features is provisional but based on a study of errors frequently made by learners of English: however, when we spot a misused preposition, it often takes some reflection to understand which elements of the sentence are making that preposition choice sound awkward, and thus we have erred on the side of generosity. In some cases it is easier: we observe that in the earlier example *England* is a location NE while *King's College* is an organisation NE: this distinction may be the trigger for the difference in preposition choice.

3 Vector construction

The features are acquired from a version of the British National Corpus (BNC) processed by the C&C tools pipeline (Clark and Curran, to appear). The output of the C&C tools pipeline, which includes stemmed words, POS tags, NER, GRs and Combinatory Categorial Grammar (CCG) derivations of each sentence, is processed by a Python script which, for each occurrence of a preposition in a sentence, creates a vector for that occurrence and populates it with *0s* and *1s* according to the absence or presence of each feature in its context. Each vector therefore represents a corpus-seen occurrence of a preposition and its context. For each preposition we then construct a dataset to be processed by a machine learning algorithm, containing all the vectors which do describe that preposition's contexts, and an equal number of those which do not: our hypothesis is that these will be sufficiently different from the 'positive' contexts that a machine learning algorithm will be able to associate the positive vectors more strongly to that preposition.

4 Testing the approach

To test our approach, we first experimented with a small subset of the BNC, about 230,000 words (9993 sentences, of which 8997 contained at least one preposition). After processing we were left with over 33,000 vectors associated with a wide range of prepositions. Of course there is a certain amount of noise: since the vectors describe what the parser has tagged as prepositions, if something has been mistagged as one, then there will be a vector for it. Thus we find in our data vectors for things such as *if* and *whether*, which are not generally considered prepositions, and occasionally even punctuation items are misanalysed as prepositions; however, these represent only a small fraction of the total and so do not constitute a problem.

Even with a relatively large number of vectors, data sparseness is still an issue and for many prepositions we did not find a large number of occurrences in our dataset. Because of this, and because this is only a preliminary, small-scale exploration of the feasibility of this approach, we decided to initially focus on only 5 common prepositions[3]: ***in** (4278 occurrences), **of** (7485), **on** (1483), **to** (4841[4]), **with** (1520)*. To learn associations between context vectors and prepositions, we use the Voted Perceptron algorithm (Freund and Schapire 1999). At this stage we are only interested in establishing whether a preposition is correctly associated with a given context or not, so a binary classifier such as the Voted Perceptron is well-suited for our task. At a later stage we aim to expand this approach so that a notification of error or inappropriateness is paired with suggestions for other, more likely prepositions. A possible implementation of this is the output of a

[1]These are 41 broad semantic categories (e.g. 'noun denoting a shape', 'verb denoting a cognitive process') to which all nouns and verbs in WordNet are assigned.

[2]Penn Treebank tagset.

[3]These prepositions often occur in compound prepositions such as *in front of*; their inclusion in the data could yield misleading results. However out of 33,339 vectors, there were only 463 instances of compound prepositions, so we do not find their presence skews the results.

[4]Here *to* includes occurrences as an infinitival marker. This is because the tagset does not distinguish between the two occurrences; also, with a view to learner errors, its misuse as both a preposition and an infinitival marker is very common.

ranked list of the probability of each preposition occurring in the context under examination, especially as of course there are many cases in which more than one preposition is possible (cf. *the folder **on** the briefcase* vs. *the folder **in** the briefcase*).

We use the Weka machine learning package to run the Voted Perceptron. Various parameters can be modified to obtain optimal performance: the number of epochs the perceptron should go through, the maximum number of perceptrons allowed, and the exponent of the polynomial kernel function (which allows a linear function such as the perceptron to deal with non-linearly separable data), as well as, of course, different combinations of vector features. We are experimenting with several permutations of these factors to ascertain which combination gives the best performance. Preliminary results obtained so far show an average accuracy of 75.6%.

5 Results and Discussion

We present here results from two of the experiments, which consider two possible dimensions of variation: the polynomial function exponent, *d*, and the presence of differing subsets of features: WordNet or NE information and the ±2 POS tag window. Tests were run 10 times in 10-fold cross-validation.

5.1 The effect of the *d* value

The value of *d* is widely acknowledged in the literature to play a key role in improving the performance of the learning algorithm; the original experiment described in Freund and Schapire (1999) e.g. reports results using values of *d* from 1 to 6, with *d=2* as the optimal value. Therefore our first investigation compared performance with values for *d* set to *d=1* and *d=2*, with the other parameters set to 10 epochs and 10,000 as the maximum number of perceptrons allowed (Table 1).

We can see that the results, as a first attempt at this approach, are encouraging, achieving a success rate of above 80% in two cases. Performance on *on* is somewhat disappointing, prompting the question whether this is because less data was available for it (although *with*, with roughly the same sized dataset, performs better), or if there is something intrinsic to the syntactic and semantic properties of this preposition that makes its use harder to pinpoint. The average performance of 75.6 - 77% is a promising starting point, and offers a solid base on which to proceed with a finer tuning of the various parameters, including the feature set, which could lead to better results. The precision and recall support our confidence in this approach, as there are no great differences between the two in any dataset: this means that the good results we are achieving are not coming at the expense of one or the other measure.

If we compare results for the two values of *d*, we note that, contrary to expectations, there is no dramatic improvement. In most cases it is between less than 1% and just over that; only *on* shows a marked improvement of 4%. However, a positive trend is evident, and we will continue experimenting with variations on this parameter's value to determine its optimal setting.

5.2 The effect of various feature categories

As well as variations on the learning algorithm itself, we also investigate how different types of features affect performance. This is interesting not only from a processing perspective - if some features are not adding any useful information then they may be disregarded, thus speeding up processing time - but also from a linguistic one. If we wish to use insights from our work to assist in the description of preposition use, an awareness of the extent to which different elements of language contribute to preposition choice is clearly of great importance.

Here we present some results using datasets in which we have excluded various combinations of the NE, WordNet and POS tag features. The WordNet and POS macrocategories of features are the largest sets - when both are removed, the vector is left with only 31 features - so it is interesting to note how this affects performance. Furthermore, the WordNet information is in a sense the core 'lexical semantics' component, so its absence allows for a direct comparison between a model 'with semantics' and one without. However, the WordNet data is also quite noisy. Many lexical items are assigned to several categories, because we are not doing any sense resolution on our data. The POS tag features represent 'context' in its most basic sense, detached from strict syntactic and semantic considerations; it is useful to examine the contribution this type of less sophisticated information can make.

	d=1				**d=2**			
Preposition	%correct	Precision	Recall	F-score	%correct	Precision	Recall	F-score
in	76.30%	0.75	0.78	0.77	76.61%	0.77	0.77	0.77
of	83.64%	0.88	0.78	0.83	84.47%	0.87	0.81	0.84
on	65.66%	0.66	0.65	0.65	69.09%	0.69	0.69	0.69
to	81.42%	0.78	0.87	0.82	82.43%	0.81	0.85	0.83
with	71.25%	0.73	0.69	0.70	72.88%	0.73	0.72	0.73
av.	75.65%	0.76	0.75	0.75	77.10%	0.77	0.77	0.77

Table 1: The effect of the *d* value

	All features	**No W.Net**	**No POS**	**No NER**	**No WN + POS**	**GRs only**
% correct	83.64%	83.47%	81.46%	83.33%	81.00%	81.46%
Precision	0.88	0.89	0.76	0.88	0.74	0.93
Recall	0.78	0.76	0.91	0.77	0.94	0.68
F-score	0.83	0.82	0.83	0.82	0.83	0.78

Table 2: OF: the effect of various feature categories (d=1)

Full results cannot be presented due to space restrictions: we present those for 'of', which are representative. In almost case, the dataset with all features included is the one with the highest percentage of correct classifications, so all features do indeed play a role in achieving the final result. However, among the various sets variation is of just 1 or 2%, nor do f-scores vary much. There are some interesting alternations in the precision and recall scores and a closer investigation of these might provide some insight into the part played by each set of features: clearly there are some complex interactions between them rather than a simple monotonic combination.

Such small variations allow us to conclude that these sets of features are not hampering peformance (because their absence does not in general lead to *better* results), but also that they may not be a major discriminating factor in preposition choice: grammatical relations seem to be the strongest feature - only 18 components of the vector! This does not imply that semantics, or the immediate context of a word, play no role: it may just be that the way this data is captured is not the most informative for our purposes. However, we must also consider if something else in the feature set is impeding better performance, or if this is the best we can achieve with these parameters, and need to identify more informative features. We are currently working on expanding the feature set, considering e.g. subcategorisation information for verbs, as well as experimenting with the removal of other types of features, and using the WordNet data differently. On the other hand, we also observe that each macrocategory of features does contribute something to the final result. This could suggest that there is no one magic bullet-like feature which definitely and faultlessly identifies a preposition but rather, as indeed we know by the difficulties encountered in finding straightforward identification criteria for prepositions, this depends on a complex interrelation of features each of which contributes something to the whole.

6 Evaluation and related work

6.1 Error detection evaluation

One of our motivations in this work was to investigate the practical utility of our context models in an error detection task. The eventual aim is to be able, given a preposition context, to predict the most likely preposition to occur in it: if that differs from the one actually present, we have an error. Using real learner English as testing material at our current stage of development is too complex, however. This kind of text presents several challenges for NLP and for our task more specifically, such as spelling mistakes - misspelled words would not be recognised by WordNet or any other lexical item-based component. Furthermore, often a learner's error cannot simply be described in terms of one word needing to be replaced by another, but has a more complex structure. Although it is our intention to be able to process these kinds of texts eventually, as an interim evaluation we felt that it was best to focus just on texts where the only feature susceptible to error was a preposition. We therefore devised a simple artificial error detection task using a corpus in which errors are artificially inserted in otherwise correct text, for which we present interim results (the dataset is currently quite small) and we compare it against a 'brute force' baseline, namely using the recently released Google n-gram data to predict the most likely preposition.

We set up a task aimed at detecting errors in the use of *of* and *to*, for which we had obtained the best results in the basic classification tests reported earlier, and we created for this purpose a small corpus using BBC news articles, as we assume the presence of errors there, spelling or otherwise, is extremely unlikely. Errors were created by replacing correct occurrences of one of the prepositions with another, incorrect, one, or inserting *of* or *to* in place of other prepositions. All sentences contained at least one preposition. Together with a set of sentences where the prepositions were all correct, we obtained a set of 423 sentences for testing, consisting of 492 preposition instances. The aim was to replicate both kinds of errors one can make in using prepositions[5].

We present here some results from this small scale task; the data was classified by a model of the algorithm trained on the BNC data with all features included, 10 epochs, and *d=2*. If we run the task on the vectors representing all occurrences of each of the prepositions, and ask the classifier to distinguish between correct and incorrect usages, we find the percentage of correct classifications as follows:

Prep	Accuracy	Precision	Recall
of	75.8	0.72	0.68
to	81.35	0.76	0.74
Average:	78.58	0.74	0.71

These results show both high precision and high recall, as do those for the dataset consisting of correct occurrences of the preposition and use of another preposition instead of the right one: (*of* - 75%, *to* - 67% - these are accuracy figures only, as precision and recall make no sense here.) This small task shows that it is possible to use our model to reliably check a text for preposition errors.

However, these results need some kind of baseline for comparison. The most obvious baseline would be a random choice between positive and negative (i.e. the context matches or does not match the preposition) which we would expect to be successful 50% of the time. Compared to that the observed accuracies of 75% or more on all of these various classification tasks is clearly significant, representing a 50% or more reduction in the error rate.

However, we are also working on a more challenging baseline consisting of a simple 3-gram lookup in the Google n-gram corpus (ca. 980 million 3-grams). For example, given the phrase *fly _ Paris*, we could decide to use ***to*** rather than ***at*** because we find 10,000 occurrences of *fly **to** Paris* and hardly any of *fly **at** Paris*. In a quick experiment, we extracted 106 three-word sequences, consisting of one word each side of the preposition, from a random sample of the BBC dataset, ensuring each type of error was equally represented. For each sequence, we queried the Google corpus for possible prepositions in that sequence, selecting the most frequent one as the answer. Despite the very general nature of some of the 3-grams (e.g. *one of the*), this method performs very well: the n-gram method scores 87.5% for *of* (vs. our 75.8%) and 72.5% for *to* (vs. our 81.35%). This is only a suggestive comparison, because the datasets were not of the same size: by the time of the workshop we hope to have a more rigorous baseline to report. Clearly, unless afflicted by data sparseness, the raw word n-gram method will be very hard to beat, since it will be based on frequently encountered examples of correct usage. It is therefore encouraging that our method appears to be of roughly comparable accuracy even though we are using no actual word features at all, but only more abstract ones as described earlier. An obvious next step, if this result holds up to further scrutiny, is to experiment with combinations of both types of information.

6.2 Related work

Although, as noted above, there is much research being carried out on prepositions at the moment, to the best of our knowledge there is no work which takes an approach similar to ours in the task of preposition choice and error correction, i.e. one that aims to automate the process of context construction rather than relying on manually constructed grammars or other resources such as dictionaries (cf. TPP). Furthermore, much current research seems to have as its primary aim a semantic and functional descrip-

[5]A third, omitting it altogether, will be accounted for in future work.

tion of prepositions. While we agree this is a key aspect of preposition use, and indeed hope at a later stage of our research to derive some insights into this behaviour from our data, at present we are focusing on the more general task of predicting a preposition given a context, regardless of semantic function.

With regard to related work, as already mentioned, there is no direct comparison we can make in terms of learning preposition use by a similar method. One useful benchmark could be results obtained by others on a task similar to ours, i.e. error detection, especially in the language of non-native speakers. In this case the challenge is finding work which is roughly comparable: there are a myriad of variables in this field, from the characteristics of the learner (age, L1, education...) to the approach used to the types of errors considered. With this in mind, all we can do is mention some work which we feel is closest in spirit to our approach, but stress that the figures are for reference only, and cannot be compared directly to ours.

Chodorow and Leacock (2000) try to identify errors on the basis of context, as we do here, and more specifically a ± 2 word window around the word of interest, from which they consider function words and POS tags. Mutual information is used to determine more or less likely sequences of words, so that less likely sequences suggest the presence of an error. Unlike ours, their work focuses on content words rather than function words; they report a precision of 78% and a recall of 20%. Our precision is comparable to this, and our recall is much higher, which is an important factor in error detection: a user is likely to lose trust in a system which cannot spot his/her errors very often[6]. Izumi et al. (2004) work with a corpus of English spoken by Japanese students; they attempt to identify errors using various contextual features and maximum entropy based-methods. They report results for omission errors (precision 75.7%, recall 45.67%) and for replacement errors (P 31.17%, R 8%). With the caveat that we are not working with spoken language, which presents several other challenges, we note that in our task the errors, akin to replacement errors, are detected with much more success. Finally we can note the work done by Eeg-Olofsson and Knutsson (2003) on preposition errors in L2 Swedish. Their system uses manually crafted rules, unlike ours, and its performance is reported as achieving a recall of 25%. On the basis of this brief and by no means exhaustive overview of the field, we claim that our results in the error detection task are competitive, and we are working on fine-tuning various parameters to improve them further.

[6]Although of course precision is a key measure: it is not helpful for the user to be exposed to false alarms.

7 Conclusion

We have presented an automated approach to learning associations between sentence contexts and prepositions which does not depend on manually crafted grammars and achieves a success rate of up to 84.5%. This model was tested on a small set of texts with artificially created preposition errors, and was found to be successful at detecting between 76% and 81% of errors. Ongoing work is focusing on how to further improve performance taking into consideration both the parameters of the voted perceptron algorithm and the feature set of the vectors.

Acknowledgements

We wish to thank Stephen Clark for stimulating discussions and the anonymous reviewers for their helpful comments. Rachele De Felice is supported by an AHRC scholarship.

References

Ted Briscoe, John Carroll, and Rebecca Watson. 2006. The second release of the RASP system. In *COLING/ACL-06 Demo Session*, Sydney, Australia.

Martin Chodorow and Claudia Leacock. 2000. An unsupervised method for detecting grammatical errors. In *NAACL-00*, Seattle, Washington.

Stephen Clark and James Curran. To appear. Wide-coverage Efficient Statistical Parsing with CCG and Log-linear Models.

Jens Eeg-Olofsson and Ola Knutsson. 2003. Automatic grammar checking for second language learners - the use of prepositions. In *Nodalida-03*, Reykjavik, Iceland.

Yoav Freund and Robert E. Schapire. 1999 Large margin classification using the perceptron algorithm. *Machine Learning* 37:277-296

Emi Izumi, Kiyotaka Uchimoto, and Hitoshi Isahara. 2004 SST speech corpus of Japanese learners' English and automatic detection of learners' errors. *ICAME* 28:31-48

Ken Litkowski and Orin Hargraves. 2005. The Preposition Project. In *Second ACL-SIGSEM Prepositions Workshop*, Colchester, UK.

Guido Minnen, John Carroll, and Darren Pearce. 2001 Applied Morphological Processing of English. *Natural Language Engineering* 7(3):207-223

Simple Preposition Correspondence: A problem in English to Indian language Machine Translation

Samar Husain, Dipti Misra Sharma, Manohar Reddy
{samar@research.iiit.net,dipti@mail.iiit.net,
manohar@students.iiit.net}
Language Technologies Research Centre,
IIIT, Hyderabad, India.

Abstract

The paper describes an approach to automatically select from Indian Language the appropriate lexical correspondence of English simple preposition. The paper describes this task from a Machine Translation (MT) perspective. We use the properties of the head and complement of the preposition to select the appropriate sense in the target language. We later show that the results obtained from this approach are promising.

1 Introduction

The task of identifying the appropriate sense from some target language (here, Hindi and Telugu) for a given simple preposition in some source language (here, English) is rather complex for an MT system, and noting that most foreign language learners are never able to get a firm hold on prepositions of a new language (Brala, 2000), this should not be surprising. A simple example illustrates the problem:

(1a) *He bought a shirt* ***with*** *tiny collars.*
'with' gets translated to *vaalii* in Hindi (hnd).
and as *kaligi unna* in Telugu (tlg).
(1b) *He washed a shirt* ***with*** *soap.*
'with' gets translated to *se* in hnd.
and as *to* (suffixed to head noun) in tlg.

For the above English sentences, if we try to swap the senses of '*with*' in their corresponding target translation, the resulting sentences either become ill-formed or unfaithful to their English source. The pervasive use of preposition (or its equivalent in a given language) in most of the languages makes it a crucial element during translation. Inappropriate sense selection of a preposition during machine translation can have a negative impact on the quality of the translation, sometimes changing the semantics of the sentence drastically, thereby making the preposition sense selection module a critical component of any reliable MT system.

Finding the proper attachment site for the preposition in English, i.e. getting the correct parse for the prepositional phrase (PP) is a classic problem in MT, and this information can be used to identify the sense of a preposition. Figure 1 and Figure 2 below show the correct attachment site of PPs in example (1a) and (1b) respectively.

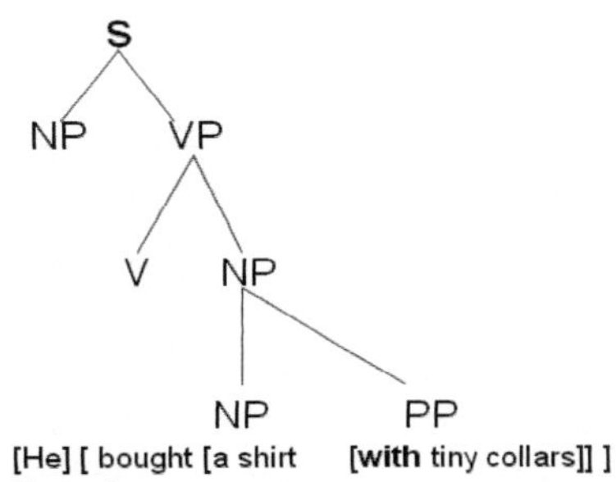

Figure 1

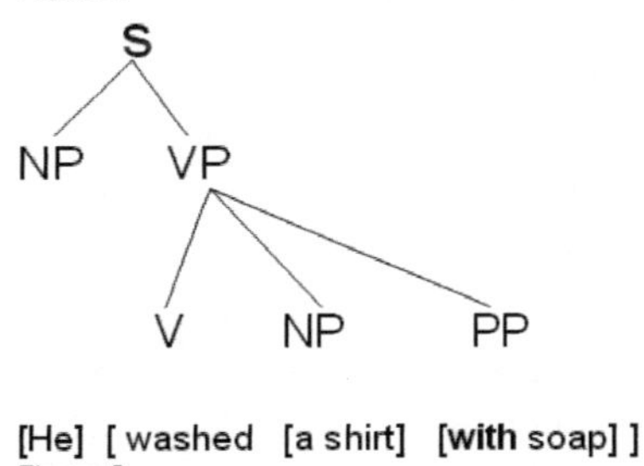

Figure 2

Proceedings of the 4th ACL-SIGSEM Workshop on Prepositions, pages 51–58,
Prague, Czech Republic, June 2007.

The correct parse of the PP helps us in selecting the appropriate sense. However, finding the appropriate attachment only reduces the problem. It does not lead to a 'complete solution'. The following examples (2a, 2b and 3a, 3b) have the same attachment site but take different senses in the target language:

(2a) *He has had fever* ***for*** *two days now.*
'for' gets translated as *se* in hnd.
and as *nundi* in tlg.
(2b) *He had fever* ***for*** *two days.*
'for' gets translated as *taka* in hnd.
Not translated in tlg.

(3a) *He is going* ***to*** *Delhi.*
'to' gets translated as *ko*, or preferably left untranslated in hnd.
and in tlg as *ki* (suffixed to the head noun), or may be left un-translated.
(3b) *He is going* ***to*** *his mother.*
'to' gets translated as *ke paasa* in hnd.
and *daggaraku* in tlg

After looking at cases such as (2a), (2b) and (3a), (3b) where the parse is same i.e., preposition 'for and 'to' get attached to the main verb 'have' and 'go' respectively, it is clear that we need to come up with some criterion which can help us in achieving our task.

There has been extensive work on understanding prepositions linguistically, often from various angles. Syntactically (Jackendoff, 1977; Emonds, 1985; Rauh, 1993; Pullum and Huddleton, 2002), from a Cognitive perspective (Lakoff and Johnson, 1980; Langacker, 1987; Brala, 2000), Semantically by (Saint-Dizier and Vazquez, 2001; Saint-Dizier, 2005), and the Pragmatic aspects by (Fauconnier, 1994).

The work of automatically selecting the correct sense has also received good amount of attention and there have been many attempts to solve the problem. (Japkowicz et. al, 1991) attempts to translate locative prepositions between English and French. The paper introduces the notion of 'representation of conceptualization' based in turn on (Grimaud, 1988). The paper synthesizes this idea with the thesis of ideal meaning (Herskovits, 1986). (Tezuka et. al, 2001) have tried to resolve conceptual geographical prepositions using inference rule based on cognitive maps which people have of the external world. (Hartrumpf et al., 2005) use knowledge representation formalism for PP interpretation.

Some studies pertain to systems which have been implemented for MT; (Gustavii, 2005) uses aligned parallel corpora to induce automatic rules by applying transformation-based learning. (Alam, 2004) make use of contextual information to determine the meanings of *over*. (Trujillo, 1992) use a transfer rule based approach to translate locative PP-phrase, the approach uses the dependency relations marked as indices with individual word and a bilingual lexicon which has mapping between source and target lexical item (with indices). (Naskar and Bandyopadhyay, 2005) look at the semantics of the head noun of the reference object (this is their main criterion) to get the lexical meaning of prepositions in an English-Bengali MT system.

The current paper presents a study of prepositions at, for, in, on, to and with in context of English to Indian language MT system. The paper is arranged as follows; Section 2 describes our approach to solving the mentioned task, the 3rd section shows the performance of our approach along with the error analysis during the testing phase, we conclude the paper along with some future direction in section 4.

2 Our Approach

All the previous attempts can be broadly classified into 3 main categories; *one*, where the preposition is the main focus, concentration is on the semantics (cognitive or lexical) of the preposition; *second*, focus on the verb and the PP which the verb takes as argument; and *lastly*, the head noun of the PP becomes the deciding factor to get the appropriate sense.

Very few approaches, like (Alam, 2004; Saint-Dizier and Vazquez, 2001), consider both, the head (modified) and the complement (modifier) information, to decide the sense of the preposition. The modified (or head) is the head of the phrase to which the PP attaches. The modifier (or complement) is the head noun of the PP. The following examples show very clearly why given a preposition we cannot depend only on the modified or the modifier separately, and that we must consider them both to solve the problem.

Considering only the modifier (the complement);

(4a) *He apologized* ***to*** *his mother.*
'to' gets translated as *se* in hnd
& *ki* (suffixed to the head noun) in tlg
(4b) *He went* ***to*** *his mother.*
'to' gets translated as *ke paasa* in hnd
& as *daggaraku* in tlg

Considering only the modified (the head);

(5a) *He waits for her* ***at*** *night.*
'at' gets translated as *meM* in hnd
& not translated in tlg
(5b) *He waits for her* ***at*** *the station.*
'at' gets translated as *par*
& as *lo* in tlg

Only considering the modifer *'his mother'* in 4a and 4b is not sufficient, likewise taking only the modified *'waits'* in 5a and 5b will be insufficient, both the pairs take different senses and have the same partial contextual enviornment which is misleading. Hence, the combined context of complement-head forms a better candidate for solving the problem. We come across plenty of cases where isolated information of modifier/modified can be misleading.

The task of preposition sense selection can be divided into;

(a) Getting the correct parse (the task of PP attachment, identification of phrasal verb, etc.),
(b) Context and semantic extraction,
(c) Sense selection.

This paper describes the algorithm for achieving the above mentioned steps. *We assume the input to our module has the correct parse, i.e. Step (a) above is assumed here.* The proposed algorithm is a component in English to Indian language MT system[1], therefore, the required input can be presumed to be available. Steps (b, c) above are rule based, which make use of the modifier-modified relation, these relations and the properties of modifier/modified form the core of the context in step (b). We then apply a series of rules, which specify the context and semantics in which a sense is expected to occur.

2.1 Context and semantic extraction

Extraction of context and semantic information (of modifier/modified) is done automatically by various sub-modules which are combined together to perform the overall task. We use the word *'context'* very loosely. A context for us is a combination of various properties which can be syntactic or lexical, or both; syntactic context can be modifier-modified relation, lexical properties can be morphological information such as TAM (tense, aspect and modality) of a verb, class of the verb (Levin, 1993), category of the lexical item and in some cases the lexical item itself.

The semantics of the modifier and the modified are captured using WordNet (Miller, 1990), and certain other resources such as person, place dictionaries, place and time filters (these filters make use of syntactic cues to mark basic time and place), etc. We use WordNet to get the hypernyms of a word. By using this property we can easily get the broader, more general class/concept for a modifier/modified. Although effective and very intuitive, this method has its own problems. We will elaborate these problems in section 3.2. WordNet is also used to identify person and place names by using the hyponym tree for person and place.

Along with the WordNet, as mentioned above, we use certain other filters such as place and time. They are used prior to using WordNet. In case a rule requires the modifier to be a *place* (rules are explained in 2.2), this information is acquired from the place filter. If the filter's result is negative we use WordNet. Dictionaries and POS tags are checked for identifying proper names, we use a proper name dictionary as POS taggers tend to have a fixed upper limit especially when it comes to the identification of named entities. In essence, the linguistic resources are used in the following order;

(1) Dictionaries,
(2) Time & Place filter,
(3) WordNet.

Preliminary results have shown that certain prepositions occurring in the PP complement of certain verb classes (Levin, 1993) translate to a specific sense in Hindi. For example, preposition 'at' in the case of *peer* verbs always translates to *kii tarapha* or *kii ora* in Hindi. This knowledge can

[1] (http://shakti.iiit.ac.in). Note here that the proposed algorithm has been tested with Shakti version 0.83x which has still not been released. The released version is 0.73.

be very informational and we plan to pursue this aspect in the future.

2.2 Sense Selection

We have noticed in the previous examples that the prepositions from English either get translated as suffixes to the head noun of the PP (in Telugu) or as postpositions (in Hindi and Telugu). An example where a preposition in English gets translated as postposition in its Telugu translation is shown below;

(6) *The book is **on** the table.*
'buka taibila ***paiina*** undi'
'Book' 'table' 'on' 'there'

We select the correct sense of the preposition based on a series of rules which are applied linearly. These rules have been manually constructed. We have tried to make the rules mutually exclusive, so that there are no clashes. Also, by making sure that the rules are mutually exclusive we don't need to worry about the order in which the rules are listed out in the rule file, thus making the rule file less fragile. These rules currently cover around 20 high frequency English prepositions, these prepositions vary in their degree of ambiguity; some are highly ambiguous (e.g. to, by, with, etc.), whereas some are less ambiguous (e.g. against, around, as, etc.), hence these are easier to handle.

Various senses on the target side for a given English preposition are selected on the basis of rules listed out in a file. The rule file comprises of tuples, each having 6 attributes.

The attributes are listed below;

a) Source Language preposition
b) Modified category
c) Constraints on the modified item
d) Modifier category
e) Constraints on the modifier item
f) Dictionary sense id of the source language preposition

An example of a tuple:
 # at, v, -, n, place_close, at%p%5

(7) *He has opened a school **at** his home.*
'usane apne ghara ***mem*** eka skuula kholaa hei'
'He *erg*' 'his' 'house' 'at' 'one' 'school' 'open' 'is'

The rule above requires the modifier to be a noun and places a constraint "place_close" on it. We map this constraint (place_close) with some set of lexical items found in a synset of a hypernym obtained from WordNet. For example, "place_close" might correspond to 'housing', 'lodging', 'building', etc in a synset. In essence "place_close" is place holder for different relations which might be present in a synset. The modified category and the modifier category can be extracted after the correct parse of the PP is known; the constraints applied on the modified and modifier item (point c, e above) can be of various kinds, some of them are;

- Semantic relations corresponding to WordNet hypernyms for a given word
- Presence of the lexical item in some list (eg. verb class)
- Semantic property such as 'time' or 'place'
- Lexical property such as aspect, negativity etc.

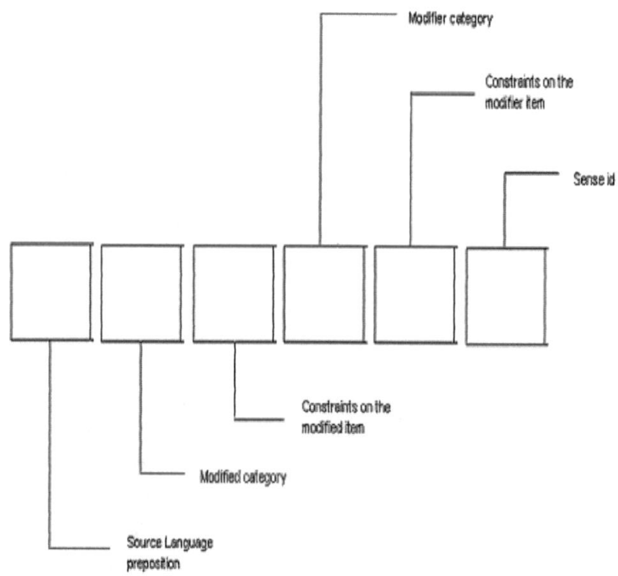

Figure 3: Single rule tuple

The constraints specified in a tuple can be combined together using logical operators such as 'and', 'or', 'negation'. So, for a single rule, multiple constraints can be introduced. For a sense, if needed, complex constraints can be introduced which must be satisfied.

#for, v, L[2]:for.dat && aspect:continuous, n, time, for%p%5

(8) *He has been playing* ***for*** *years.*
'vaha kaii saalo ***se*** khela rahaa hai '
'He' 'many' 'years' 'for' 'play' 'cont.' 'is'

The above rule (for the Hindi translation) has two constraints for the modified (which is a verb in this case), the two constraints have been combined using an 'and' operator (represented using two ampersands, '&&'). Only if the two constraints are satisfied, the constraint is considered as satisfied else it is considered as failed. The use of different logical operator gives a lot of expressive power to a single rule. Sometimes it might be desirable to place multiple constraints together, because for a given sense these constraints always occur together, and by listing them as separate rules we will miss out the fact that they co-occur.

It is not always necessary (or possible) to fill the constraint fields. In fact, sometimes it is even desirable to leave them unspecified. In such a case we place a hyphen in that field, such as the following rule;

 # at, v, -, n, place_close, at%p%5

In the above rule, the constraint for the modified field is unspecified. There are also cases when it is not desirable to have a translated preposition corresponding to its source;

 # to, L: verbs.txt, -, n, place, ZZ

(9) *He went* ***to*** *Delhi.*
'vaha dilli gayaa' (in hnd)
'He' 'Delhi' 'went'

The 'ZZ' in the above rule signifies that the translated sentence will have no preposition corresponding to the preposition 'to' when it occurs with certain verbs which are specified by "L:verbs.txt" ('verbs.txt' is a list of verbs). For the above Hindi sentence post-position 'ko' can perhaps be introduced, i.e. 'vaha dilli ***ko*** gayaa', but 'vaha dilli gayaa' is more natural, and the translated sentence is better off without a 'ko'.

[2] List

Finally, each preposition handled has a default rule, which is applied at the end when all the other rules for that preposition fail; the sense given by the default rule is based on the most frequent usage of the preposition at the target side. All the fields (except the first and last) in the default rule have hyphens. The default rule for *'to'* is written below;

to, -, -, -, -, to%p%1

Some of the rules in the rule file are given below, for ease of comprehension, we mention the actual target sense instead of the dictionary id for the last field (the actual rule file has dictionary sense id)

at, v, L:peer_verbs.txt, n, -, kii tarapha
at, v, L:transaction_verbs.txt, n, price, meM
for, v, -, n, distance, taka
in, n, animate, n, place, kaa
on, v, -, n, time, ko
to, v, L:go_verbs.txt, n, animate|authority, ke paasa
with, v, -, n, instrument, se

2.3 Recap

We briefly describe the various steps of the algorithm again;

(a) Given a raw sentence we feed it to the Shakti MT system which performs various source language analysis, for our algorithm, information such as PP attachment and correct identification of the phrasal verb (if present) is crucial.
(b) The output of step (a) is taken by our module which automatically constructs the six field tuple described above. At this point we can only fill some fields, which are field 1 (source language preposition), field 2 (modified category) and field 4 (modifier category).
(c) We then compare this constructed tuple with the appropriate tuples present in the rule file. For this constructed tuple to satisfy the various constraints mentioned in the tuple with which it is compared resources such as place filter, time filter, lists and WordNet are consulted automati-

cally. The order in which we use these resources has been already been mentioned in section 2.1. The tuple for which all the constraints are satisfied is selected, the last field of this tuple contains the dictionary id of the sense.

(d) Output the selected sense.

3 Evaluation

For the current study, experiments were conducted with 6 high frequency prepositions, they are; *at*, *for*, *in*, *on*, *to*, and *with*. The algorithm was tested on 100 sentences for each preposition in both the language pairs, i.e., 600 sentences for English-Hindi and 600 sentences for English-Telugu. These sentences were randomly extracted from the ERDC[3] corpus. The corpus contains text from different domains such as medicine, sports, history, etc. The input to the implemented system was manually checked and corrected to make sure that there were no errors in the information which is expected by the system. The bulk of these corrections involved rectifying the wrong PP attachment given by the parser and the mistakes in phrasal verb identification.

Prep[4]	Precision	BL	No. of Sense
At	73.4	51.5	5
For	84.05	69.5	6
In	82	65.2	7
On	85	70	3
To	65.2	35.4	10
With	66	50	6

Table 1{English-Hindi}.

Prep[4]	Precision	BL	No. of Sense
At	68	48	5
For	72	50	7
In	82	82	3
On	76	76	2
To	80	80	2
With	94	90	3

Table 2{English-Telugu}.

[3]Electronic Research and Development Centre, NOIDA

[4] Prepositions

3.1 Performance

The tables above show the performance of the system and compares it with the baseline score (BL). BL is the precision of the system with only the default sense. The tables also show the number of sense which English prepositions can take on the target side. Table 1 and Table 2 show English-Hindi and English-Telugu results respectively.

The implemented system gives very promising results. Certain prepositions give comparably low precision. The reasons for the inappropriate sense selection are discussed in the next section. The English-Telugu results (Table 2) show same system precision and BL for some preposition ('in' and 'to'). This is because these prepositions have less number of sense on the target side and all the instances found in the test data had the default sense.

3.2 Error analysis

The errors made by the system were analyzed and the major reasons for inappropriate sense selection were;

(a) Noise generated by WordNet,
(b) Special constructions,
(c) Metonymy,
(d) Ambiguous sentences,
(e) Presence of very general constraints.

The problem of noise generation by WordNet sometimes leads to surprising and unexpected sense selection; this is because in WordNet a noun or verb will have multiple sense, and each of these senses will have various levels of hypernym synsets, so, while finding various concepts/features (specified by the rule for a preposition) we need to look at each one of these senses. We need to do this because we currently don't have the sense information. So, an inappropriate sense might sometimes satisfy the constraint(s) and result in inappropriate selection. The solution for this will obviously be to identify the correct sense of modifier/modified prior to getting its semantic property from the WordNet.

There are certain constructions in which the head noun of the PP is a pronoun, which refers back to a noun. For us this will create a problem, in such cases we will first need to get the referent noun and then apply the constraints on it, take the following example;

(10) *The rate at which these reactions occur is known as rate of metabolism.*

In the above example, the head noun of the PP (*at which*) refers to the noun (*rate*) on which we need to apply the constraints. At present the coreference information is not available to us, therefore in such cases the algorithm fails to give the correct output.

The other reason for failure was the ambiguity of the sentence itself which could be interpreted in various ways, like the example below;

(11) *Andamaan should go to India.*

The above sentence can be interpreted (and translated) in two ways, the hindi translations for the two interpretation are;

(11a) '*andamaan indiaa ko jaanaa chahiye*'
'Andamaan' 'India' 'to' 'go' 'should'
India should get Andaman.

(11b) '*andamaan ko indiaa jaanaa chahiye*'
'Andamaan' 'to' 'India' 'visit' 'should'
Andaman should visit India.

In (11a) we get the sense that the possesion/control of 'Andamaan' should go to 'India', and in (11b) it is 'Andamaan' (the government of 'Andamaan') which is going to 'India' (the government of India), as in, *The United States should go to UK*, also in (11b) we can have 'Andamaan' as somebodys' name, as in, *Ram should go to India.* In such cases we failed to get the appropriate translation of the preposition as it in turn depends on the correct interpretation of the whole sentence. Ambiguity of numerals in a sentence is yet another case which lead to faliure, like the following example;

(12) *At 83, Vajpayee is overweight.*

In the above sentence, the number 83 can either mean this persons' (*Vajpayee*) age or his weight. The target side translation takes different preposition sense for these two interpretation. Hindi takes *para* and *in* Telugu 'at' is not-translated when we treat 83 as weight, and when treated as age, we get *mem* and *lo/ki* in Hindi and Telugu respectively.

We found that certain prepositions occur in large number of metonymical usage, like, 'with' and 'at'. The constraints in a rule have been formulated for the general usage and not the extended usage of a given word. The example below shows one such instance;

(13) *Great bowlers spend hours after hours at the nets.*

While looking in WordNet for the various senses of 'net' not a single sense matches with the kind of usage in which 'net' is used in the above sentence.

Certain rules for some of the preposition were found to be very general, the low performance of 'for' and 'to' in telugu and hindi respectively are mainly due to this reason. In general, formulating rules (English-Hindi) for preposition 'to' was very difficult. This was because 'to' can have around 10 senses in Hindi. The rules with very general constraints tend to satisfy cases where they should have failed. One has to revisit them and revise them.

4 Conclusion and Future Work

In this paper we described an approach to select the appropriate sense for a preposition from an English to Indian language MT perspective, we discussed the issues involved in the task, we explained the steps to achieve the required task; which are, semantic and context extraction, and sense selection. We reported the performance of the system, and showed that our approach gives promising results. We also discussed the identified problems during the error analysis; such as noise generation by WordNet.

One of the pertinent tasks for the future would be to come up with a solution to reduce the noise generated by WordNet. The scope of rule file in terms of handling more prepositions needs to be broadened. We would like to extend this work to handle complex preposition. Finally, we would like to explore if ML techniques can be combined with the rule base to exploit the benefits of both the approaches.

References

Yukiko Sasaki Alam. 2004. Decision Trees for Sense Disambiguation of Prepositions: Case of Over. In *HLT/NAACL-04.*

Marija M. Brala. 2000. Understanding and translating (spatial) prepositions: an exercise in cognitive semantics for lexicographic purposes.

Joseph Emonds. 1985. *A unified theory of syntactic categories.* Dordrecht: Foris.

Gilles Fauconnier. 1994. *Mental spaces.* Cambridge: Cambridge University Press.

M. Grimaud. 1988. Toponyms, Prepositions, and Cognative Maps in English and French, *Journal of American Society of Geolinguistics.*

Ebba Gustavii. 2005. Target Language Preposition Selection - an Experiment with Transformation-based Learning and Aligned Bilingual Data. In *Proceedings of EAMT 2005.*

Sven Hartrumpf, Hermann Helbig and Rainer Osswald. 2005. Semantic Interpretation of Prepositions for NLP Applications. In *EACL 2006 Workshop: Third ACL-SIGSEM Workshop on Prepositions*

A. Herskovits. 1986. *Language and Spatial Cognition, An Interdisciplinary Study of Prepositions in English.* Cambridge University Press.

Cliffort Hill. 1982. Up/down, front/back, left/right. A contrastive study of Hausa and English. In *Weissen born and Klein,* 13-42.

Ray Jackendoff. 1977. *The architecture of the language.* Cambridge, MA: MIT Press.

Nathalie Japkowicz and Janyce M. Wiebe. 1991. A System For Translating Locative Preposition From English Into French. In *Proc. Association for Computational Linguistics.*

George Lakoff and Mark Johnson. 1980. *Metaphors we live by.* Chicago: University of Chicago Press.

Beth Levin. 1993. *English verb classes and alternations.* Chicago/London: The University of Chicago-Press.

George A. Miller. 1990. WordNet: An online lexical database. *International Journal of Lexicography.*

Sudip Kumar Naskar and Sivaji Bandyopadhyay. 2005. Handling of Prepositions in English to Bengali Machine Translation. In *EACL 2006 Workshop: Third ACL-SIGSEM Workshop on Prepositions.*

Geoffrey Pullum and Rodney Huddleston. 2002. Prepositions and prepositional phrases. In *Huddleston and Pullum (eds.),* 597-661.

Gisa Rauh. 1993. On the grammar of lexical and nonlexical prepositions in English. In *Zelinskiy-Wibbelt (eds.),* 99-150.

Patrick Saint-Dizier and Gloria Vazquez. 2001. A compositional framework for prepositions. In *IWCS4, Tilburg, Springer*, lecture notes, p. 165-179.

Patrick Saint-Dizier. 2005. PrepNet: A framework for describing prepositions: Preliminary investigation results. In *Proc. of IWCS 6*, Tilburg.

Joseph M. Sopena, Agusti LLoberas and Joan L. Moliner. 1998. A connectionist approach to prepositional phrase attachment for real world texts. In *COLING-ACL '98*, 1233-1237.

T. Tezuka, R. Lee, H. Takakura, and Y. Kambayashi. 2001. Web-Based Inference Rules for Processing Conceptual Geo-graphical Relationships. In *Proc. of the 2nd Int. Conf. on Web Information Systems Engineering, The 1st Int. Workshop on Web Geographical Information Systems.*

Arturo Trujillo. 1992. Locations in the machine translation of prepositional phrases. In *Proc. TMI-92.*

Author Index

Association for Computational Linguistics
209 N. Eighth Street
Stroudsburg, Pennsylvania 18360